Designing for disabled children and children with special educational needs

Guidance for mainstream and special schools

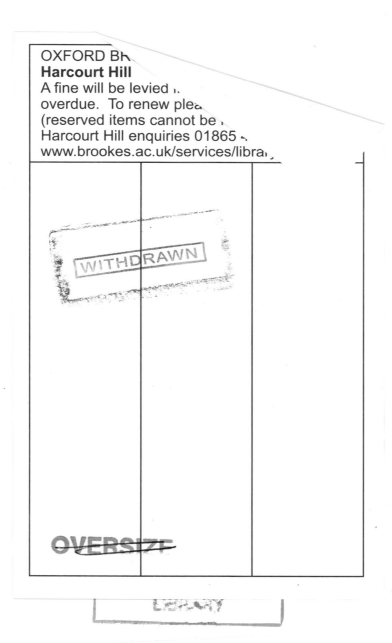

**department f
children, sc**

D1382239

Contents

A Background and briefing

B The design approach

Acknowledgements

The publication was prepared by the following team:

Gill Hawkins	DCSF
John Jenkins	Haverstock Associates
Lucy Watson	DCSF
Val Foster	Val Foster Associates
Malcolm Ward	Malcolm Studio
Daniel Keeler	PB&R Design Services, Hampshire County Council

DCSF would like to thank the following for their help and advice:

Kathie Bull	Educational consultant
Steve Clow	PB&R Design Services, Hampshire County Council
Brian Coapes	Centre for Healthcare Architecture and Design, NHS Estates
Mike Collins	NAS
Angela Duncan	Headteacher, Meadows School, Sandwell
David Gardiner	HMI
Susan Logan	BRE
Lucy Naish	RNIB
Susan Peace	Qequality – Promoting Quality Service for Disabled People
Nick Peacey	SENJIT
Sue Roberts	Headteacher, Cornfield School, West Sussex
Caroline Roaf	NASEN
Philippa Russell	Council for Disabled Children
Steve Sands	Hunters
Jane Simpson	Jane Simpson Access Ltd
Shirley Turner	Education officer
Richard Vaughan	NDCS
Terry Waller	Becta

We are also grateful to the following schools and their architects for welcoming visitors and/or providing us with information:

Arbourthorne Community Primary - Sheffield
Astley Sports College &
Community High School - Tameside
Baytree Community Special School - Somerset
Beaconside CofE Infant School - Penrith
Braidwood School for the Deaf - Birmingham
Castlegreen Community School - Sunderland
Columbia Grange School - Sunderland
Cromwell Community High School - Tameside
Filsham Valley - East Sussex
Fox Hollies Special School - Birmingham
Fulford School - York
Greenfields School - Northampton
Hazelwood School - Glasgow
Heritage Park Community School - Sheffield
Hollywater School - Hampshire

Manor Green Primary School - West Sussex
North Lakes School - Cumbria
The Meadows School - Birmingham
The Michael Tippett School - Lambeth
The Orchard School - Sandwell
The Phoenix School - Grantham
Osborne School - Hampshire
Portland School - Sunderland
Priestley Smith School - Birmingham
Reignhead Primary School - Sheffield
Shepherds Down Special School - Hampshire
Springwell Dene School - Sunderland
Stephen Hawking School - Tower Hamlets
St Giles School - Retford
Ullswater Community College - Cumbria

Introduction

The Government's aim is that by 2020 we want England to be the best place in the world to grow up. That includes providing every child and young person with learning opportunities and challenges which build their confidence and self esteem and set them on the road to a fulfilling future as a UK citizen.[1]

The Children Act 2004 provides the legal framework for the Government's national change programme, Every Child Matters – Change for Children. It requires all partner agencies to work together to improve five key outcomes for all children and young people, including those with special educational needs (SEN) and disabilities:

- Be healthy
- Stay safe
- Enjoy and achieve
- Make a positive contribution
- Achieve economic well-being

The Department for Children, Schools and Families (DCSF) has a continuing commitment to improving provision for disabled children and children with SEN in mainstream schools and special schools. The Primary Capital Programme and Building Schools for the Future (BSF) are a unique opportunity to transform our schools and provide innovative learning environments that will support and inspire pupils to achieve. This includes improving special school provision, most of which will be re-built or refurbished by 2020.

Schools vary in the facilities and specialist services they offer. The needs of children with SEN and disabilities are met by schools working in partnership with parents, with other schools (sometimes as part of a co-located campus) and with the NHS and other children's services.

Schools are a vital community resource. By 2010 all schools will be providing access to a range of extended services - childcare in primary schools, parenting support, swift and easy referral to targeted and specialist services, and wider community access to IT, sports and arts facilities, including adult learning. Designing for disabled children and those with SEN is an essential part of this extended community focus.

New arrangements for 14–19 year olds require schools and other providers to work together in partnerships, many of which build on earlier collaborative arrangements. No institution acting alone will be able to provide the full 14–19 offer to their learners. Schools, colleges, training providers, employers and other stakeholders will have to collaborate, focusing on what they do best to deliver the curriculum. School design needs to take account of a school's role in local partnership arrangements, the particular contribution that the school makes, the additional pupils who may be using school facilities and the extra movement between sites that may be involved.

Children and young people need attractive, accessible school buildings. 'Inclusive' design can enable and empower those with SEN and disabilities to participate fully in life at school and in the wider community.

This building bulletin draws together information to help everyone involved in designing these schools to work together to produce good quality, sustainable school premises that support the achievement of the five Every Child Matters outcomes, are inspiring and uplifting, and pleasant and convenient for everyone to use.

1. Refer to:
The Children's Plan: Building brighter futures DCSF 2007 – http://www.teachernet.gov.uk/educationoverview/briefing/current-strategy/childrensplan/

Scope

This publication sets out non-statutory guidance on planning and designing accommodation for new and existing schools in England – all of which will have at least some children or young people with SEN and disabilities.

This building bulletin supersedes and replaces:

• Building Bulletin 77: Designing for Pupils with Special Educational Needs, Special Schools 1992

• Building Bulletin 91: Access for Disabled People to School Buildings 1999

• Building Bulletin 94: Inclusive School Design 2001

Who this publication is for

This publication is for all local authorities (LAs), diocesan boards of education, governing bodies of schools and all other education providers.

It has been written particularly for education advisers, architects and designers, and may also be useful to building contractors on school building projects, school/PRU managers, and managers in other children's services.

Table 1: Definitions
Special educational need (SEN)
'A child has SEN if he (or she) has a learning difficulty which calls for special educational provision to be made for him (or her).' Section 312 of the Education Act 1996
Disability
'A disabled person is someone who has a physical or mental impairment which has a substantial and long-term adverse effect on his or her ability to carry out normal day-to-day activities.' Disability Discrimination Act 1995 **NB** A child may be covered by both the SEN and DDA definitions.
Terminology
The term 'children' is used throughout this document to cover very young children in early years settings and pupils of statutory school age (5-16 years old) attending schools. 'Young people' is used for post-16 students. Current usage favours the phrasing 'disabled children and children with special educational needs'. However, this guidance also uses 'children with SEN and disabilities'.

How to use this publication

The publication is structured so that it can be used for designing and building for any phase of education, mainstream or special. For mainstream schools the guidance should be read in conjunction with Building Bulletins 98 and 99[2].

If you are improving or remodelling existing buildings, you will find it a useful guide for bringing accommodation up to current standards.

It can also be used to inform the development of school accessibility plans and disability equality schemes, to plan to improve access for disabled people to schools over time.

It is not meant to be prescriptive but instead to offer guidelines that will result in inclusive environments for all children with SEN and disabilities. Designs should always evolve through close consultation with schools, SEN experts and local authorities, based on local need.

The bulletin is divided into six parts, which should each inform the design and build:

Part A: Background and briefing
– sets out the essential information underpinning design for children and young people with SEN and disabilities:

- the context and special educational provision
- children's SEN and disabilities
- meeting children's needs
- planning building projects, including the process and the briefing contents

Part B: The design approach
– addresses whole school design issues and 'inclusive' design principles which should underpin all elements of design for children with SEN and disabilities. These principles should be used as a reference for any project of this kind.

Part C: Designing school spaces
– looks in more detail at specific spaces and covers:

- what needs to be included in designs for children with SEN and disabilities
- key design points
- charts showing area guidelines

NB The middle section of Part C is divided by phase of education. The guidance in these pages can be put together to suit the age range of any school.

Part D: Detail development
– focuses on what is relevant for school building projects for children with SEN and disabilities, including:

- building construction
- environmental services
- furniture, fittings and equipment (FF&E) and ICT

Part E: Case studies
– the case studies illustrate many of the points raised in other sections of this book and show some of the wide range of approaches to meeting the needs of children with SEN and disabilities.

Part F: Annexes
– sets out further detailed information on legal aspects, education accessibility, as well as typical model schedules of accommodation for special schools.

2. Refer to:
Building Bulletin 98:
Briefing Framework
for Secondary School
Projects
and
Building Bulletin 99,
Briefing Framework for
Primary School Projects –
http://www.teachernet.
gov.uk/sbareaguidelines/

Background and briefing A

This part looks first at the needs of children with SEN and diabilities – crucial for designers and specifiers to understand from the outset. It goes on to examine the initial process for a school building project and developing a brief.

1. Understanding SEN and disability

Context

Almost a fifth of children in Britain are identified as having special educational needs (SEN). It is estimated that around 7 per cent of children are disabled and a significant number of children have both SEN and a disability[1].

Most children with SEN and disabilities are educated in mainstream schools. Around one per cent of the total school population is educated in special schools.

The Government wants to ensure that every child with SEN and disabilities gets an education that allows them to achieve their full potential. Where a child has SEN, a school's statutory duties include doing its best to ensure that the necessary provision is made for them and that they join in school activities with other pupils as much as possible.

Under the Disability Discrimination Act 1995 (as amended by the Disability Discrimination Act 2005) (DDA), every local authority and school must:

• not discriminate against disabled pupils – they must not treat them 'less favourably' and must actively make 'reasonable adjustments' to ensure that they are not at a substantial disadvantage

• plan strategically to increase access for disabled pupils to the curriculum, improving the physical environment so that disabled pupils can take advantage of the education and services offered, and improving information for disabled pupils – they need to show in their accessibility plans how they will do this. (See Annex A, Legal framework.)

• promote equality of opportunity for disabled people

Local authorities (LAs) are required to produce a Children and Young People's Plan, which is a single, strategic, overarching plan for all services affecting children and young people[2].

When they are proposing any change to provision for children with SEN, LAs (and others) must demonstrate their application of the SEN Improvement Test to parents, the local community and decision makers, showing how the proposed alternative arrangements are likely to lead to improvements in the standard, quality and/or range of educational provision for children with special educational needs.

1. Refer to: Prime Minister's Strategy Unit report, Improving the Life Chances of Disabled People, 2005 – http://www.cabinetoffice.gov.uk/strategy/work_areas/disability.aspx

2. Refer to: http://www.everychildmatters.gov.uk/cypp/

Special educational provision

A variety of provision is needed in each area to address the range of need. Provision is likely to include:

Mainstream schools – where most children with SEN are educated. The Children's Plan says that mainstream schools can and should be providing high quality support for the vast majority of children with SEN and disabilities. Working collaboratively with specially resourced provision, with support services and special schools, mainstream schools can ensure that the wide spectrum of SEN is met.

Resourced provision – where places are reserved at a mainstream school for children with a statement for a specific type of SEN. Children are taught mainly within mainstream classes but there is usualy also a base and/or some specialist facilities around the school.

Designated unit – where children with a statement for a specific type of SEN are taught wholly or mainly in separate classes provided within a mainstream school.

Special schools – organised specifically for children with a statement for a specific type of SEN.

Co-location – where children with a statement are educated in separate special school facilities with separate staff but on the same site as a mainstream school. There should be some interchange of pupils, resources, staff and dual use of facilities.

Dual registration enables some children with SEN and disabilities to attend mainstream and special schools part time. Schools can also work together in partnerships, clusters or federations.

Outreach, support and training
Many schools run outreach services, particularly special schools and mainstream schools with resourced provision or a designated unit. Some schools also operate in-reach services where pupils and or staff from other schools come on site to access specialist facilities or expertise within the school. Many schools with specialist expertise or facilities also provide training. Some schools provide a base for SEN support services. An understanding of the school's role in the pattern of local provision and the range of functions that it fulfils for pupils, parents and professionals is crucial to an understanding of the design requirements.

Sometimes, LAs may place children in independent or non-maintained special schools. See Annex C, page 188, for more details.

Children's special educational needs and disabilities

The SEN Code of Practice stresses the importance of not assuming hard and fast categories of SEN. Each child is unique and there is a wide spectrum of special educational needs, although there are also specific needs that usually relate directly to particular types of impairment. Children with SEN and disabilities have needs and requirements which may fall into at least one of four areas:

- Cognition and learning
- Behavioural, emotional and social
- Communication and interaction
- Sensory and/or physical

Many children have inter-related needs. For example, a pupil with general learning difficulties may also have a sensory impairment. Disabled children, however, do not necessarily have SEN. The largest group of pupils who may count as disabled under the DDA but do not necessarily have SEN are those with particular medical conditions.

3. For more information refer to Chapter 3 of the SEN Code of Practice 2001 – http://www.teachernet. gov.uk/wholeschool/sen/ sencodeintro/

Cognition and learning

Children may demonstrate features of moderate, severe or profound learning difficulties or specific learning difficulties, such as dyslexia. Some may have associated sensory, physical and behavioural difficulties that compound their needs. Some may be on the autistic spectrum.

Children who have these needs require specific strategies to help their learning and understanding. These may include strategies to support the development of language, literacy and organisational skills and practical sensory or physical experiences to support the development of abstract ideas and concepts.

Behaviour, emotional and social development

Children who have behavioural, emotional and social difficulties may be withdrawn or isolated, disruptive and disturbing and they may be hyperactive. They may lack concentration and have immature social skills. Challenging behaviour may arise from other complex special needs.

Children who have these needs may require a structured learning environment, with clear boundaries for each activity. They may need extra space to move around and to ensure a comfortable distance between themselves and others. They may take extreme risks or have outbursts and need a safe place to calm down. Behaviour support or counselling may take place in a quiet supportive environment.

Table 2: Main types of SEN[3]

Cognition and learning	
Specific learning difficulty	SpLD
Moderate learning difficulty	MLD
Severe learning difficulty	SLD
Profound and multiple learning difficulty	PMLD
Behaviour, emotional and social development	
Behaviour, emotional and social difficulty	BESD
Communication and interaction	
Speech, language and communication needs	SLCN
Autistic-spectrum disorder	ASD
Sensory and/or physical	
Hearing impairment	HI
Visual impairment	VI
Multi-sensory impairment	MSI
Physical disability	PD

Communication and interaction

Most children with special educational needs have strengths and difficulties in one, some or all of the areas of speech, language and communication. The range of difficulties will encompass children with a speech and language impairment or delay, children with learning difficulties, those with a hearing impairment and those who demonstrate features within the autistic spectrum.

Children with these needs require support in acquiring, comprehending and using language, and may need specialist support, speech and language therapy or language programmes, augmentative and alternative means of communication and a quiet place for specialist work.

Children with autistic spectrum disorder have difficulty interpreting their surroundings and communicating and interacting with others. They need an easily understood environment with a low level of distraction and sensory stimulus to reduce anxiety or distress. They may need a safe place to calm down.

Sensory and/or physical needs

There is a wide spectrum of sensory, multi-sensory and physical difficulties. Sensory needs range from profound and permanent deafness or visual impairment through to lesser levels of loss, which may only be temporary. For some children these needs may be accompanied by more complex learning and social needs.

Children with these needs require access to all areas of the curriculum and may use specialist aids, equipment or furniture. Many will need specialist support (for example mobility training or physiotherapy).

Children with sensory impairments may need particular acoustic or lighting conditions. Some may need extra space and additional 'clues' to help them negotiate their environment independently.

Children with physical disabilities may use mobility aids, wheelchairs, or standing frames, which can be bulky and require storage. Whether they are able to move around independently or need support, there should be sufficient space for them to travel alongside their friends. Accessible personal care facilities should be conveniently sited.

Health and personal care needs

Pupils with a range of medical needs may count as disabled under the DDA and may or may not have accompanying special educational needs. They may need facilities where their medical or personal care needs can be met in privacy.

Meeting children's needs

Understanding the range of ways in which children's needs are met will help ensure that the spaces designed for them are suitable.

Curriculum and learning

Children with SEN and disabilities take part in learning activities appropriate to their age and phase of education, with activities and materials that may be 'differentiated', with tasks adapted for individuals. A range of teaching approaches and learning styles is used, along with a variety of activities, including academic, vocational, ICT (information and communication technology) and multi-sensory.

Teaching and learning approaches vary and may involve thematic and cross-curricular work. For example, food technology may combine English, maths and science, as well as life skills and personal, social and health education. Access to outdoor learning is essential for science, physical education, sensory experiences and mobility training.

Groups in special schools/units are considerably smaller than in mainstream schools.

Learning social skills helps children with SEN and disabilities take a fuller part in daily life. Dining together is an integral part of their curriculum and some children have additional support for this.

Promoting health and well-being is important – children with SEN and disabilities take part in physical exercise through games or sports (sometimes adapted to suit needs), adventure play and mobility training, as well as through recreational and social activities.

Older children are likely to need access to careers advice and work-related experiences. Some may follow vocational courses, which may be arranged at further education colleges or at other schools for part of the young person's timetable.

Groupings and staffing

Children with SEN and disabilities in mainstream schools tend to be taught with their peers in groups of up to 30 with one teacher, depending on the children's age, needs and sometimes ability. There may also be small group and one-to-one work with support staff and/or specialist teachers.

Where there are children in special classes or in special schools, group sizes (with one teacher) may range between:

- eight and 15 children with moderate needs
- six and eight children with severe to profound needs
- four and six children with profound needs only

Ways of grouping children also vary. Children with a wide range of SEN and disabilities can be grouped together if their needs allow it. But those with, for example, severe or profound learning difficulties, who need stimulation, are likely to be grouped separately from children with autism, who need low sensory stimulus.

Children who are boisterous or aggressive, such as children with behavioural, emotional and social difficulties attending a unit or special school, may be taught separately from those who are vulnerable.

Teaching assistants and support staff work alongside the teacher with individual children or with groups, in the same room or a separate space. A SENCo (SEN Co-ordinator) supports children with SEN in a mainstream school. Visiting professionals, such as a speech and language therapist, may work with particular children. Some children have high level needs and require a great deal of assistance from a large number of support staff.

In mainstream schools children may have additional support in small groups or 1:1.

Additional support

- **Learning support** – extra learning support can be provided by reducing numbers in a class, by having specific groupings or settings within that class, or by working separately in small groups or one to one with extra staff.

- **Behaviour support** – for some children this is about learning to communicate and develop social skills. For others, it means support or counselling in a separate quiet space that has a balance between privacy and visibility for supervision.

- **Learning aids, ICT and specialist furniture, fittings and equipment** – a variety of learning tools and teaching resources, ICT (computers and access technologies), specialist aids and equipment are used, some of which are bulky. Children may need particular furniture, fittings and equipment, such as height adjustable workstations.

- **Therapy** – therapies such as speech and language therapy, physiotherapy or hydrotherapy are used, particularly in special schools. Drama, art, music and movement can also be used as therapy in addition to provision through the mainstream curriculum.

- **Multi-sensory stimulation** – multi-sensory interactive work uses communication and language techniques, tactile and practical tasks, music and movement, specialist ICT, and light or sound technology or resources.

- **Personal support and care** – children with complex health needs may have medical, healthcare and/or social support from specialist support staff. Designs need to ensure they can be treated with dignity and respect, and enable support for their family and carers.

Additional support may include: one-to-one learning and behaviour support (a); physiotherapy (b); use of specialist ICT hardware (c); multi-sensory work (d).

a

b

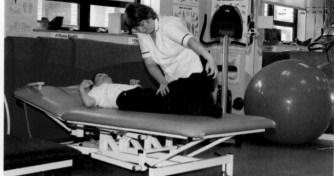

c

d

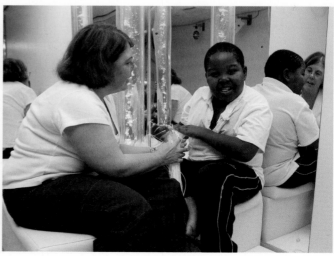

2. Planning building projects for children with SEN and disabilities

It is important to think about children's SEN and disabilities right from the start, placing them at the heart of all stages in the design process.

The process

Whatever the scale and scope – whether minor works, remodelling or building a new school – the project will involve the following:

Establishing roles and responsibilities

Roles and responsibilities need to be set out clearly from the start, identifying who has overall legal responsibility, who approves expenditure, and who has authority to give instructions. All those involved must be clear of the client's role.

This guidance assumes that the client for a building project is the local authority (LA); but the client might equally be a school governing body or other provider, such as a non-maintained special school, an independent school or diocesan board.

Making initial investigations

The client finds out what is needed[4] and whether any approvals are required, taking into account:

- the current and likely future needs of children, young people and adults with SEN and disabilities

- the results of consultations about re-organisations or SEN provision and the SEN Improvement Test

- how the school or facility fits into the local pattern of provision

- national and local policies and initiatives, such as the Children and Young People's Services Plan, disability equality schemes, LA accessibility strategy, and school accessibility plans

- plans for transport, sustainability plans and school premises

- general accessibility both to buildings and opportunities, including Disability Discrimination Act (DDA) compliance

Making an initial statement of requirements

The strategic needs, objectives, cost budgets and constraints are identified through consultation with, for example, LA officers responsible for education, SEN provision, children's services, buildings, disability or access.

Setting up a project team

The client appoints architects and engineers for design, quantity surveyors for costs, a CDM (Construction, Design and Management) co-ordinator for health and safety, a SEN or access adviser, and a client design adviser. Appointing an experienced SEN design team can add significant value during the briefing and formative stages of a project.

Ensuring sufficient funding

It is particularly important for the client to secure sufficient funding and resources so that children's needs can be met and good practice standards reached or exceeded[5]. Projects for special schools and designated units, especially where children have high level needs, may require significantly more funding than for other school building projects. The LA may need to join up funding from different budgets for shared use facilities and have other funding to support other services where extra accommodation is provided, such as a health centre.

4. Refer to: DCSF guidance Planning and Developing Special Educational Provision – http://www.dcsf.gov. uk/schoolorg/

5. A school governing body undertaking a project with their own funds should consult the LA on approvals.

Achieving value for money

The project must achieve value for money. There often needs to be a balance struck between 'realistic needs' and 'wish lists' in order to keep costs within the project cost plan. However, access and inclusion for children with SEN and disabilities should always remain a high priority.

New build versus refurbishment

The viability of each must be explored at the outset by means of a costed feasibility study. The impact of work on an occupied campus, taking on board the level of disabilities, should also be assessed and agreed with the school.

Developing a good quality brief

The briefing process overlaps with the inception, feasibility study and initial concept design stages of a project. The brief itself provides a clear framework for consultation and discussion.
It sets out in writing the purpose and scope of the project, along with the main requirements and performance outcomes for the school buildings and grounds, forming the basis of the work to be carried out by the project design team[6].

As the design evolves, the brief is developed through discussion between the client, the project team, various specialists and stakeholders:

- LA officers in SEN and disability, building or children's services

- health professionals, therapists and relevant professional bodies

- disability organisations

- technical specialists

- subject specialists

- parents, carers and children

Consultation is a vital part of the briefing process and sufficient time must be allowed for it. A carefully constructed brief, based on detailed discussion and consultation, helps to ensure good quality accommodation

6. Refer to:
Inclusive Projects – best practice advice on the process of delivering an inclusive environment, DIPTAC – http://www.dptac.gov.uk/

that is fit for purpose, meeting children's learning and social needs and supporting their health and well-being. This phase may involve testing and re-testing ideas or scenarios to meet the type and range of children's needs to be catered for at the school. It is often useful for school staff and the design team to visit recently completed or exemplar schemes to inform their decisions.

The final brief describes the detailed requirements for all spaces, to be agreed by the client.

Monitoring progress

The access requirements for people with SEN and disabilities need to be checked with stakeholders at every stage and reviewed regularly throughout the design and build process. The client should appoint someone to oversee project progress and make sure the brief is met.
Once agreed, the project should be monitored for good quality design, construction and maintenance. It is advisable to make sure there is an audit trail recording and giving reasons for any changes made.

Co-location

These projects need plenty of time for proper collaboration and planning. What spaces will be shared? How will staff be organised? It may be useful to visit other co-located schools to gain a better understanding of what works well and how the two schools interact.

Consulting stakeholders

Make sure stakeholders are involved throughout the briefing and design process and that they are:

- involved at the right time
- well prepared and given the relevant issues so their contribution is useful
- kept informed about the impact of their involvement. Information may need to be provided in different formats to ensure inclusion.

Properly supported by staff, children with SEN and disabilities can contribute to the brief through classroom discussions and activities.

Children at The Meadows special secondary school, Sandwell, for example were involved in:

- choosing colours
- designing the school emblem
- producing a newsletter

all of which helped their transition to the new building and fostered a sense of belonging.

At the Michael Tippett special school, Lambeth, architects Marks Barfield worked very closely with staff, organising site visits to exemplary schools to inspire them and gauge what would and wouldn't work for them. A viewing gallery – specially adapted for pupils with special needs and disabilities – was set up to allow children to visit the site during construction. This provided a learning opportunity for both pupils and staff and enabled them to get ready for the move and change to their environment. An interactive architectural model of the school also increased staff and pupils' engagement with the move to their new school.

Cost of building for children with SEN and disabilities

- The costs of providing additional support spaces, resourced provision and designated units varies locally. Where they are planned as part of a new-build school project, the same cost allowances as for mainstream schools may be adequate.

- For small new-build extensions, the cost rates increase greatly due to the higher proportion of structure and services (roof, wall and floor) as a ratio to their internal floor area.

- Major refurbishment works may cost almost as much as new build; minor works to existing premises may prove cost effective.

- Some special school projects are more costly because they are for a small number of pupils with a high level of needs. Some of these schools require more robust specialist materials, safety and security systems. Others need mobility equipment and hydrotherapy pools.

- Where additional provision in mainstream schools is similar to that in special schools, cost rates may increase accordingly.

Briefing contents

Putting together an effective brief involves looking at the bigger picture, combining aspiration and practicality[7]. The guidance below is written with a particular emphasis on special schools/units, but the principles apply to any project for children with SEN and disabilities.

The project vision

The vision should describe the school ethos and/or educational vision to be reflected in the design. For example, to support children's:

- learning experiences
- health, safety, welfare and well-being
- participation in school life
- outcomes and life chances

Children with SEN and disabilities share aspirations with their peers and want to use the same range of facilities. The practical issues that may arise need to be tackled in a way that does not detract from the children's everyday experience.

School organisation and management

Each school has its own timetable and plan for the school year and school day, reflecting its ethos and educational vision. It is often useful to explain in detail a typical school day, school activities and any other services during and out of school hours. This should include any arrangements for sharing facilities with other schools, for example through 14–19 partnerships.

Planned occupancy

Figures should include the overall school population, taking account of both current and likely future needs, explaining how each group uses the premises, broken down by:

For children:

- each class or year group, their age, key stage and/or phase of education

- children's SEN and disabilities, focusing especially on any particular needs that are being planned for
- arrangements for dual placements, visiting children or groups and/or for access to learning elsewhere
- the approach to meeting these and any potentially different needs, where these entail different accommodation requirements.

For staff:

- teaching, support, administration and maintenance, full-time, part-time and disabled staff
- visiting professionals, outreach and multi-agency staff
- extended school and community staffing
- any on-site training needs for school and visiting staff

For visitors:

- parents, siblings, support workers or carers, including disabled people
- users of the school facilities and services, including disabled people

Learning and social needs

A curriculum analysis or study of the timetabled and non-timetabled spaces helps ensure effective use of space, including:

Curriculum and mode of delivery:

- subjects taught, teaching methods and curriculum activities
- degree of differentiation from mainstream provision
- early developmental work/learning experiences and specialist activities in relation to abilities and need
- learning aids, specialist equipment, ICT, access technology, services and storage
- learning and behaviour support and SEN specialist, medical and therapy facilities and storage

7. Refer to: Briefing Details at www.nbseducator.co.uk/briefs

A Client Guide to Developing School Buildings RIBA 2007 – http://www.ribabookshops.com

The Design Quality Indicator (DQI) for Schools provides a framework for the assessment of school design. In the initial stages it is used to help a group of stakeholders form a consensus about priorities – http://www.dqi.org.uk/schools/

Teaching and learning groups:

• type, number and size for each subject or learning activity

• children's type and range of needs, staffing details and the sessions for types of support

Facilities, services and spaces

For any school, the brief should describe for each space:

• size, shape, proportion, aspect, materials, finishes and room relationships

• subject resources, display, learning aids, furniture, hoisting, fittings and equipment, layout and storage

• lighting, heating, ventilation, acoustics, communications, and services

Schedule of accommodation[8]

The brief should include a 'schedule of accommodation', listing all spaces, indoors and out, typically:

a range of learning and social spaces including:

• class bases or general teaching spaces

• learning resource spaces, small spaces for learning and/or behaviour support

• practical spaces, taking into account health and safety require-ments, accessible layout and specialist equipment

• spaces for music and drama

• large spaces for movement and sport, assembly, performance and inclusive dining

• accessible outdoor spaces – for curriculum use (outdoor classroom, nature trails, PE activities), social/recre-ational use, and SEN therapy/training (sensory gardens, mobility trails)

SEN and disability specialist support spaces including:

• medical facilities

• therapy and support spaces according to needs, such as for physi-otherapy, sensory learning, counselling, and social skills development

a range of other support spaces, including:

• staff spaces, including for outreach and training and for visiting professionals (allowance should also be made for parents)

• necessary stores and maintenance services – for all spaces and to accommodate mobility aids

• accessible toilets and changing spaces for personal care – for disabled children and adults, independent or assisted, at convenient intervals around the school

• kitchen spaces for the type of catering chosen

Allowance should be made for any shared or dedicated space for extended school services, multi-agency working or community use.

Schedule of furniture and equipment

A schedule of furniture and equipment needs to be drawn up, detailing furniture, fittings and equipment for each space. It is essential to work in close consultation with SEN experts, the school and other key stakeholders so that the schedule reflects the use of the space and the needs of the people using it.

Impact of evolving legislation and regulations

The design team should identify emerging legislation and regulations and new technologies to ensure the completed project is compliant in all respects.

8. The list of spaces in Annex E provides a useful checklist for putting together a schedule of accommodation.

The design approach

Part B sets out 'inclusive design' principles, which put children with SEN and disability at the heart of the design. It then looks at key issues to address at the early stage of planning the site and its buildings. Detailed design and specification are covered in Parts C and D and should be read in conjunction with these sections.

3. Inclusive design principles for schools

An attractive, accessible school environment promotes a sense of belonging and self-worth.
Inclusive school design goes beyond a one-size-fits-all model, considering all users and addressing any barriers that might deny anyone - children with SEN and disabilities, disabled staff and visitors – access to services. (See Annex A for legal requirements and non-statutory guidance.) It may mean providing more than the norm.

The design principles that follow define the key characteristics that help to achieve inclusive environments. Many of these principles overlap and in a few cases conflict, so designers need to take an holistic and coordinated approach to the design solution.

Access

An accessible environment helps children with SEN and disabilities take part in school activities alongside their peers. School designs should ensure:

- a simple, clear layout, easily understood by all users (See page 31.)
- accessible circulation routes, broad enough for people using wheelchairs or sticks (See Circulation, page 41 and Doors, page 145.)
- ergonomic details (such as door handles) that mean everyone can use them
- means of escape designed to take account of disabled people

Space

Some children with SEN and disabilities need more space – for moving around for example (some with mobility aids), for using specialist equipment, for communicating, and for 'personal' space. There needs to be room for:

- safe vehicular movement (which could be considerable in a special school)
- safe clearances around furniture and equipment, especially for wheelchair users
- additional staff working in learning and support spaces
- storage and use of (sometimes bulky) equipment and a wide range of teaching resources

Sensory awareness

Designers should take account of the varying impact of a school's environment on children's sensory experience. For example, designers should consider:

• appropriate levels of glare-free controllable lighting (See page 149.)

• good quality acoustics, taking into account the needs of people with sensory impairments and/or communication and interaction needs (See page 149.)

• visual contrast and texture, which can be used for sensory wayfinding (See page 147.)

• reduced levels of stimuli, (for example, avoiding sensory overload for a child with autism) to provide a calming background to learning

• sensory elements - using colour, light, sound, texture and aroma therapeutically, in particular for children with complex health needs

Enhancing learning

A well-designed environment enhances the educational experience for all children, including those with SEN and disabilities. Designers need to consider:

• teachers and children being able to communicate clearly

• accessible workstations with space for learning aids and assistants alongside

• furniture, fittings and equipment that support a range of learning and teaching styles

• easy access to specialist ICT resources, personal belongings, aids and mobility equipment

B

Photo Andrew Lee

Texture and surface modulation on walls and markings on floors can all help children with visual impairments to find their way around the school.

Flexibility and adaptability

Schools need to be flexible for everyday use and adaptable over time to meet the current and future needs of children with SEN and disabilities. Approaches include:

• rationalising (non-specialist) spaces so their functions can change over time

• having access to different sizes of space (possibly by moveable partitions) to suit different needs

• being able to adjust the environment locally (for example, lighting) for a variety of learning needs

• minimising fixed furniture, fittings and equipment to allow re-arrangement for different activities and changing needs

• positioning structural elements and service cores (lifts, stairs and toilets or load-bearing walls) to allow future adaptation

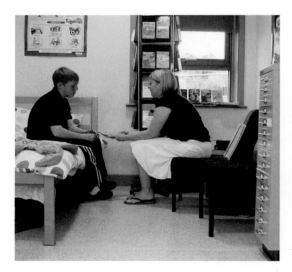

Health and well-being

Schools should promote health and well-being, dignity and respect, creating pleasant, comfortable spaces for all. This means considering school life from the perspective of the child, taking into account:

• thermal comfort, particularly for people with limited mobility or those unable to communicate their needs

• ventilation that provides good oxygen levels to avoid drowsiness or discomfort, without uncomfortable draughts

• the need to minimise disturbance from sudden or background noise

• accessible personal care facilities, provided at convenient intervals around the school and integrating them sensitively into the design

• specialist medical and therapy facilities, designed to appropriate standards

• hygiene and infection control (especially for children with lowered immunity) in relation to materials, ease of cleaning/maintenance and environmental services (See Building construction, page 139, and Environmental services, page 149.)[1]

• the outcome of health and safety risk assessments

1. It is important to establish any specific health needs of children early on and to seek specialist advice where needed.

Safety and security

All children, including those with SEN and disabilities, need to feel safe and secure, supported in their progress to independence. Levels of security required will depend on early-stage risk assessments. Designers need to consider:

- good sight lines for passive supervision, particularly where inappropriate behaviour can occur and where activities involve risk

- zoning to reflect different functions or users (See page 30.)

- minimising risk[2] of harm, without restricting the development of life skills

- **security** - preventing unauthorised access and exit without looking Institutional

Sustainability

It is vital to achieve a high quality of sustainable design. DCSF's sustainability framework states that:
'By 2020 the Government would like all schools to be models of social inclusion, enabling all pupils to participate fully in school life, while instilling a long-lasting respect for human rights, freedoms, cultures and creative expression.'
Schools should demonstrate the following:

- **Social:** having a fully inclusive and cohesive school community, with a positive relationship with the wider community and other services accessing the site

- **Economic:** achieving value for money based on the whole-life cost of the building, bearing in mind the possible higher cost of meeting some of the needs of children with SEN and disabilities and disabled adults

- **Environmental:** minimising any negative environmental impact and making good use of the site's microclimate and biodiversity, with efficient use of energy and resources, ensuring the needs of disabled people are not compromised[3]

2. Need to have regard to the outcome of health and safety risk assessments (especially where children may have risk-taking or challenging behaviour, or be unaware of risks).

3. Refer to: Environmental sustainability, page 155 and DCSF Sustainable Schools website – www.teachernet.gov. uk/sustainableschools

B

4. Initial design strategies

Site development

The following points apply particularly to a special school (whether stand-alone or co-located with a mainstream school) but should be borne in mind when any school is developed, to ensure inclusion[4]:

• The school should be conveniently located, with good transport links and proximity to other local school and community facilities, so that schools can work in partnership to support children with SEN and disabilities, and to make it easier to access work experience and training opportunities, as well as for social inclusion and local community involvement.

• The site should ideally be relatively level but changes in level can be exploited positively for split-level two-storey school accommodation, which offers external access to the ground at both levels.

• Where special schools are built on restricted sites that cannot comply with the Education (School Premises) Regulations requirements for playing fields, access to the curriculum should be ensured by partnership arrangements with other schools and centres. For more information on primary and secondary outdoor facilities, see pages 68 and 100.

• The level of security required is often higher at a special school. The following needs (sometimes conflicting) will have to be addressed:
• The level of school-time visitors (therapists, children from other schools)
• Safe means of escape
• Protection of vulnerable children, who may be unaware, for example, of traffic dangers
• Children with challenging behaviour who may climb walls, run away or cause harm

For more detail on external circulation see Access and circulation, page 38 and Building construction, page 139.

4. The development of mainstream sites is covered in Building Bulletin 98, Briefing Framework for Secondary School Projects and Building Bulletin 99, Briefing Framework for Primary School Projects – http://www.teachernet.gov.uk/sbareaguidelines/

Diagramatic site plan of a primary special school for about 60 pupils with a broad range of needs

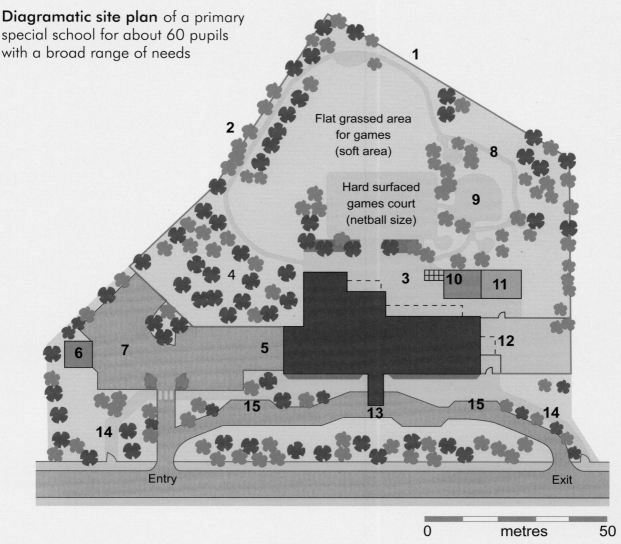

Flat grassed area for games (soft area)

Hard surfaced games court (netball size)

Entry

Exit

0   metres   50

Key

1. Red line denotes walls and fencing for safety and security
2. Shelter belt of trees and shrub planting along the site boundaries
3. Outdoor extension of class bases
4. Established copse provides habitat area
5. Deliveries and collections
6. School bus garage
7. Staff and visitors' car parking. There is likely to be more car parking space at a special school than in a mainstream school of equivalent size because of the high staffing levels and number of specialist staff visiting the site.
8. Nature trail suitable for wheelchairs
9. Sheltered hard surfaced play area
10. Greenhouse and garden
11. Play equipment in protected area with safety surface
12. Covered area to nursery/infant protected play area
13. Canopy over entrance and drop off/pick up point for taxis, cars and buses
14. Footpath to school entrance separated from access road by planting
15. Access road: It is crucial to work out the road layout for vehicles bringing non-ambulant children to the school entrance door(s) at an early stage. The area required is likely to be considerably more than at a mainstream school. (See Access and circulation, page 38.)

Planning special school buildings

The example schedules in Annex E can be used as a checklist of spaces and as a guide to gross area.

Once the range of spaces has been agreed, the area guidelines in Part C can be used to build up a fully detailed schedule of accommodation.

Rational room relationships help the whole school function well for students with SEN and disabilities and have an impact on accessibility. It is important to minimise travel distances between spaces, especially for children who have difficulty moving independently.

The diagram opposite shows typical room relationships for an all-age special school for pupils with a broad range of needs. The spaces are grouped together according to function (teaching and learning; therapy and medical; dining and social; staff/ admin).

Key points to note (most of which apply to all special schools):

- Reception/admin office is close to the main entrance.
- Spaces most used by visiting staff and parents (such as meeting/parents rooms) are easy to access from the main entrance.
- Large spaces likely to be used by the community are easy to reach but allow separation from teaching and learning spaces.
- Shared medical and therapy rooms are easy to access for all age groups.
- Small group rooms and local stores are close to teaching spaces.
- There is a progression of spaces from youngest to oldest pupils.

Zoning

Zoning can help children with SEN feel secure and make wayfinding easier. Zones reflect different functions and access by different users. For example:

- Accessible open areas and more secure areas
- Noisy and quiet areas
- 'Clean' and 'dirty' areas
- Formal and informal uses
- Areas for very young and for older children

- Toilet areas in small clusters are evenly distributed to limit travel distances.
- Outdoor spaces are easily reached, especially by younger children.
- Large spaces are adjacent, allowing them to be combined when required. Access to the outdoors needs to be well planned to maximise children's opportunities for outdoor social and learning activities.

Planning around one or more courtyards can provide calm, quiet and protective spaces that are particularly necessary for some pupils with SEN. Courtyards need to be large enough (150–300 m2) for a range of activities, with adequate sunlight, avoiding overshadowing. (A 10–12m minimum width is recommended.) A smaller courtyard 80m2 (8 x 10m) may form a sensory garden.

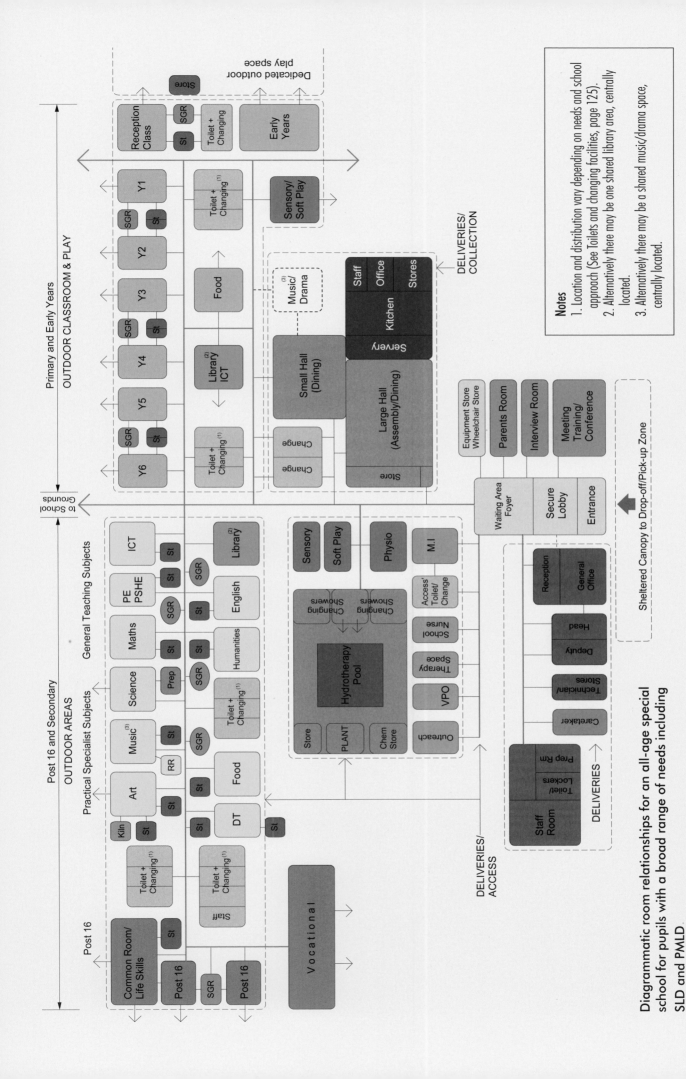

Notes

1. Location and distribution vary depending on needs and school approach (See Toilets and changing facilities, page 125).
2. Alternatively there may be one shared library area, centrally located.
3. Alternatively there may be a shared music/drama space, centrally located.

Diagrammatic room relationships for an all-age special school for pupils with a broad range of needs including SLD and PMLD.

B

Co-location

Arrangements for co-locating mainstream and special schools vary and will affect the planning of the site and its buildings. For example, there may be:

- separate identities and separate buildings
- separate identities and buildings, with some shared accommodation and resources
- a fully integrated school but with some specially resourced or designated SEN accommodation

Any shared spaces, especially for curriculum use, should be within reasonable travel distance for both groups. If the two schools are distinctly separate, there need to be safe pedestrian routes between them to facilitate sharing.

Shared social spaces can act as links or buffer spaces between the schools.

If a special school is being co-located with an existing mainstream school, it is important to check the accessibility of the existing school and make amendments accordingly. Resourced provision and designated units are generally located near well-used facilities to reduce travel time around the school (especially for children with mobility needs) and encourage social interaction (especially for children with speech, language and communication needs and behaviour, emotional and social difficulty). Quieter locations (not remote or isolated) may be needed, with safe, contained outdoor space – for example, for children with autism, or for a nurture group for young children with BESD.

All-age schools

All-age special schools should provide a sense of progression, with age-appropriate environments. Usually there are designated parts of the building for each phase of education, with their own external space and separate entrance, although there may be a central core of shared facilities, such as for therapy, administration and staff.

If an all-age special school is co-located with a mainstream primary or secondary school, any shared spaces must be suitable for the full age range of special school children.

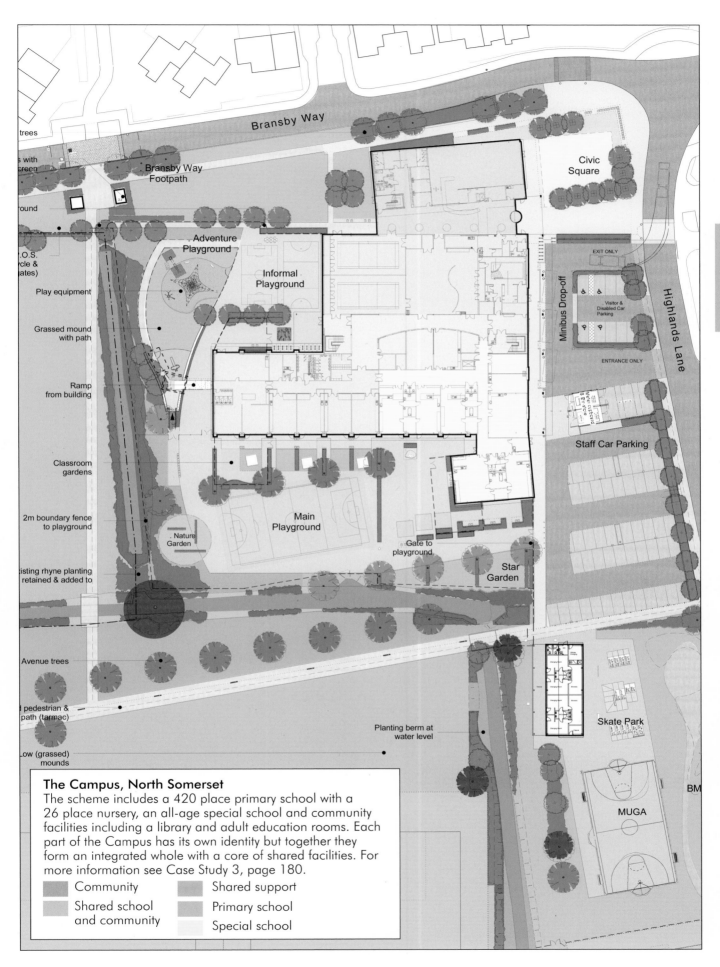

Bransby Way

Bransby Way
Footpath

trees

s with
screen

ound

.O.S.
cle &
ates)

Play equipment

Grassed mound
with path

Ramp
from building

Classroom
gardens

2m boundary fence
to playground

isting rhyne planting
retained & added to

Avenue trees

l pedestrian &
path (tarmac)

ow (grassed)
mounds

Adventure
Playground

Informal
Playground

Main
Playground

Nature
Garden

Gate to
playground

Star
Garden

Planting berm at
water level

Civic
Square

EXIT ONLY

Visitor &
Disabled Car
Parking

ENTRANCE ONLY

Minibus Drop-off

Highlands Lane

Staff Car Parking

Skate Park

MUGA

BM

B

The Campus, North Somerset

The scheme includes a 420 place primary school with a
26 place nursery, an all-age special school and community
facilities including a library and adult education rooms. Each
part of the Campus has its own identity but together they
form an integrated whole with a core of shared facilities. For
more information see Case Study 3, page 180.

	Community		Shared support
	Shared school and community		Primary school
			Special school

Designing school spaces

This part looks at designing typical spaces for children with SEN and disabilities. It begins with guidance on access and circulation, which applies to all schools. Learning and social spaces is divided by phase of education (early years, primary, secondary, post–16) and subdivided into mainstream or special schools. The guidance on support spaces includes typical specialist therapy and medical spaces in a special school (but which could be provided in any setting, depending on need).

Using Part C

This guidance can be used for any school by combining information from appropriate sections. However, school settings vary widely and it is important that school staff work closely with the design team to provide a range of spaces to suit their particular needs.

For mainstream schools, the guidance should be read in conjunction with BB99/98. The mainstream section outlines the key design issues for ensuring an inclusive environment for children with SEN and disabilities in typical mainstream spaces. It also describes typical accommodation that might be provided in addition to that specified in BB99/98 to support children with a range of needs.

For co-located schools, designers need to plan initially for the special school and then develop arrangements within the mainstream school. Curriculum analysis will establish whether it is feasible for the two schools to share spaces. There should be enough space to ensure protected timetable access for the special school and the spaces must be properly equipped to meet the children's needs. For example, the special school may have access to the mainstream school science laboratories and the mainstream school may have access to specialist support facilities such as physiotherapy or hydrotherapy. (See also Co-location, page 32.)

For all-age special schools, guidance can be drawn together from different sections as appropriate. Some spaces may be age specific, while others may be used by all. Economies of scale must not be made at the expense of access to the curriculum. Dining spaces may be used by all ages if appropriately designed and managed.

NB Technical specification is covered in Part D and should be read in conjunction with these sections.

Area guidelines

The area guidelines in these sections are a useful basis for designing school accommodation. However, it is important to note:

• For new-build accommodation, reducing the recommended floor areas is not advisable – that would restrict provision for learning and teaching, as well as flexibility and adaptability for future use.

• For existing buildings, the guidance is a useful comparison to improve accommodation and bring it in line, as far as possible, with current standards. Circumstances may limit what can be achieved, so allowances will have to be made. Any variations should be checked against health and safety risk assessments for the numbers of children and staff, activities to be carried out and the type and range of children's SEN.

• Ultimately, LAs and schools should decide the safe occupancy for a given space in relation to the number of children, the age, type and range of their needs, the number of staff, the activities to be carried out, the type and range of children's SEN, and the furniture, fittings and equipment.

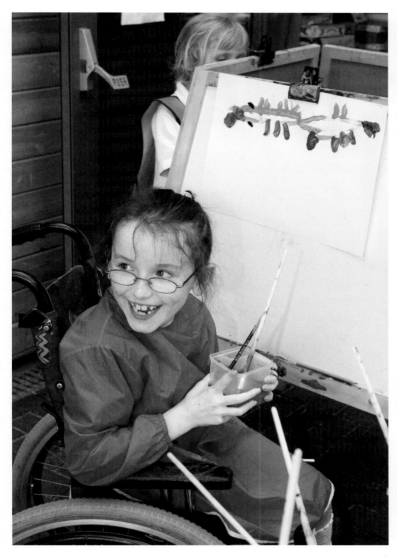

C

5. Access and circulation – all schools

Access, arrival and departure

Convenient travel routes and distances make life easier for people with SEN and disabilities, especially for those with mobility aids, sensory and learning disabilities and autism.

The exact requirements will depend on the school's particular arrangements and who will be coming to the school. Children may arrive on foot, by bicycle or buggy and may be using wheelchairs or other mobility aids. Some will use public or private transport – designers will need to find out the potential number of vehicles and process of handover to the school. In a special school particularly there may be several vehicles arriving to drop children off at the same time.

Arrival and departure take time and resources, which calls for careful operational planning (and must ensure health and safety). Transferring children in wheelchairs from the rear or side of a vehicle is a slow process, which takes place in all weathers.

The approach from gate to entrance doors should have:

- vehicular circulation that allows for public and private transport, including set-down and drop-off without congestion (for example, one way or roundabout traffic flow), and makes provision for emergency access and maintenance (See plan below.)

- designated safe pedestrian routes – some people have less awareness of the risks of traffic (or cannot see/hear vehicles) and this should be taken into account when the site is planned (a)

- easily accessible, level or ramped slip-resistant and well-drained surfaces along the route, without trip hazards and with an accessible stepped route nearby to give a choice

- suitable car parking, with accessible parking bays near the entrance (subject to local planning)

- good quality external lighting for routes, clear legible signage, visual contrast and sensory wayfinding to help independence

Plan showing the vehicular and pedestrian approach to Hollywater School. Letters refer to points in the text. Hollywater is described in more detail on page 172.

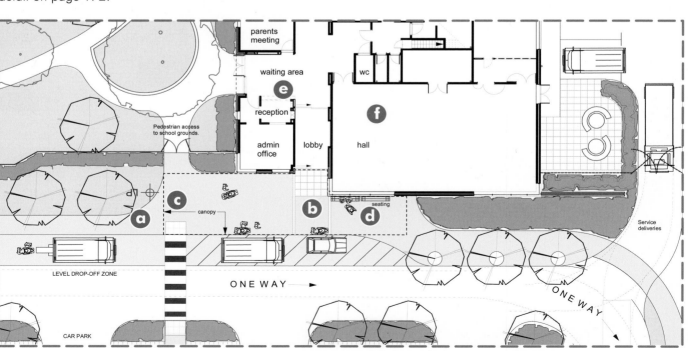

Entering the school

Children may all enter the school through the main entrance, or there could be separate entrances, depending on the way the school is organised. For younger pupils, entry might be via a gated or fenced area, with sheltered access and waiting areas.

The school building's entrance should be easily identified from a distance by its design, location, lighting and signage (tactile signs are generally not recommended for external use), and have:

• a level threshold with a safe, level drop-off zone that has, ideally, only shallow gradient ramps (b)

• a canopy or covered access to the pavement for children transferring to or from buses or taxis (without being a hazard in the route) (c)

• sheltered, accessible waiting spaces - for parents with other children, if appropriate, and for children with SEN and disabilities to wait for assistance - with a visible, easily operated entry phone or intercom to reception (d)

• easily operated doors, such as automatically operated sliding doors, with appropriate fail safe mechanisms, wide enough and in a safe and secure position (See Doors, page 145.)

• sufficient circulation space for people (including those in wheelchairs) to gather inside the building at the start and finish of the school day, avoiding congestion – safety is paramount, since this can be a particularly stressful time for some children (e and f)

• a good visual link between inside and outside, so that reception staff can oversee and supervise easily (CCTV cameras should be discreet and not detract from the welcome or reduce accessibility)

At some special schools, there may be several buses bringing children to school.

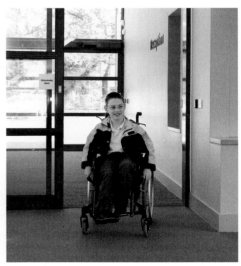

Reception/lobby/entrance area

The reception space should be attractive, friendly and welcoming, with:

• a secure, draught-free, convenient and welcoming lobby, with outer and inner doors and security controls, giving reception staff better access control (a)

• an easily identifiable reception counter, ideally facing onto the secure lobby, with a sliding window or glazed screen at an accessible height, a lower section and knee recess for wheelchair users, and a hearing loop (b)

• waiting and seating areas with sufficient space for wheelchair users or people with buggies (c)

• visual and/or tactile signage, sited where users can take time to read it (See Wayfinding, page 147.)

• appropriate good quality lighting: the entrance/reception can offer a transition lighting zone where people with visual impairments can adjust between a bright exterior and a subdued interior - the receptionist's face should be clearly visible, avoiding down-lighting that casts shadows on the face of the receptionist or visitor (See Lighting, page 149.)

• well organised safe display of children's work to promote a sense of achievement and belonging (without impeding circulation, causing hazards or obstructing lighting)

• safe storage of personal belongings and mobility equipment, with battery charging close by, so that there can be easy transition between equipment from home and school (d) (See Storage, page 121.)

• accessible toilet(s)/changing room signposted nearby (e)

• a parents' room (often) located nearby (f)

Plan of the entrance area at Hollywater School. (See photos below.) Letters refer to points in the text. Hollywater is described in more detail on page 172.

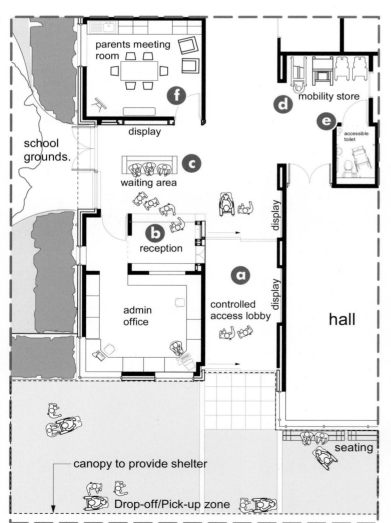

Circulation

Movement and travel are part of a learning process for many children who are developing independence skills, and they should be able to move around alongside their peers.

The aim is to plan for circulation that minimises travel distances and times. There should be a choice of routes to avoid congestion, conflict, difficult or long travel, and waiting.

Children may need different types of support or supervision and might:

• use mobility aids, frames, wheelchairs, shuffle along the floor, use a handrail for support, or have a member of staff to walk beside them

• use varied wayfinding techniques, such as signs, symbols, colour, sound, tactile cues and objects of reference to help them negotiate their environment (See Wayfinding, page 147.)

• be supported by a sighted guide or learn to use sticks or tactile routes

Co-location

Designers should consider all users. For example:

• avoiding conflicting routes between different groups

• planning busier and quieter routes

• providing passing bays or incidental or quiet spaces off routes

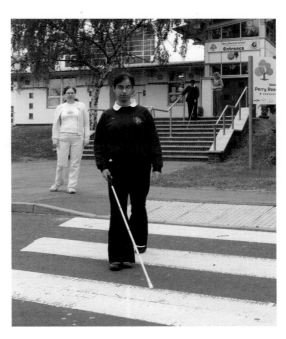

Children with visual impairment need opportunities to learn wayfinding techniques.

Some children may need the support of staff.

Outdoor circulation

Outdoor circulation needs to have a clear rationale and provide a variety of accessible routes to suit the whole spectrum of children, minimising gradients so that they can easily access all outdoor facilities.

There should be:

- shelter available along routes for more vulnerable children, with seats every 50m on long pedestrian routes

- safe and easily navigable surfaces (wheelchair accessible), with safe changes in level or transitions between surfaces - both ramps and steps[1] are needed where level access is not possible

- good sightlines for overseeing children's safety, with no hidden spaces

- noisy busy routes separate from quieter sheltered spaces, so more vulnerable children can make their own way at their own pace

- level thresholds for access by wheelchair users and to avoid staff lifting mobility equipment

- wide enough gates

- wide paths with defined edges, well away from outward opening windows (1200mm, preferably 1500mm and 1800mm for busy routes with passing places as required)

- any hazards clearly identified

1. For more detail on ramps and steps, refer to Part D and Building Regulations Approved Document M – http://www.planningportal.gov.uk/buildingregulations

Circulation space should be wide enough for wheelchair users to move around alongside their friends.

Internal circulation

Some children need more space than usual between themselves and others: a child learning how to use aids and manoeuvre equipment will need considerable clearance space; a member of staff walking beside a child with visual impairment will take up a lot of room; children with hearing impairment need space to sign and gesticulate while walking.

All circulation areas should be wide enough for wheelchair users to pass safely in different directions (avoiding long narrow corridors or 'race tracks'). This is critical where there is a high proportion of children using wheelchairs, or needing assistance from support workers. Some children may need handrails along corridors.

Approved Document M recommends that a minimum clear width in corridors for two wheelchairs passing is 1800mm (the dimension to be between handrails where provided). However, a clear width of 2m is preferable for corridors leading to more than two classrooms, with a 2.7–3m clear width in major circulation areas, particularly where there are lockers.

A simple, easily understood layout, which relates to the movement patterns dictated by the curriculum activities, makes circulation around the school easier. Any open plan spaces should allow for circulation 'routes' that minimise distraction. Designs also need to take account of emergency escape procedures (in consultation with the fire authority), incorporating the outcomes of health and safety risk assessments.

Internal circulation spaces should have a light, airy, uplifting ambience to encourage positive behaviour - displays of children's work and achievements can help with this. Changes in colour, texture or proportion can all be used to help children orientate themselves. (See Wayfinding, page 147.)

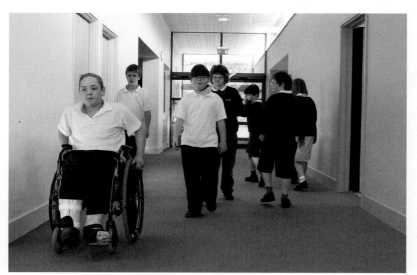

Bays off circulation routes can be provided for children to sit and talk, rest, re-orientate or calm down and let others pass – but they need to allow clear sightlines and passive supervision, since hidden spaces can encourage inappropriate behaviour.

There should be outdoor access for curriculum and social activities and for means of escape but it should be controllable for safety and security, especially where there is a possibility that children might try to run out of school. (See Fire evacuation, page 159.)

NB Special schools need greater overall area for circulation than a mainstream school – usually at least 25 per cent of the gross internal floor area.

Circulation spaces should have:

- clear signage with easily understood contrast, signs and symbols at an appropriate height

- tamper-proof fittings, no projection points, and hazards clearly identified

- good lighting and views out, but avoiding glare

- robust, easily maintained finishes

- good acoustics

- easily identified and operated, well-sited, sufficiently wide doors, with good visibility on both sides, not directly opposite or too close to other doors, to avoid congestion
(See Doors, page 159.)

Vertical circulation

Ramps, steps, stairs and lifts need to be designed to meet the current regulations and be suitable for people with SEN and disabilities. See Part D for guidance on these elements.

Climbing stairs is part of the learning process for some children.

Waiting space outside a lift should take account of nearby door openings and passing traffic.

C

6 Learning and social spaces – early years[2]

2. Refer to:
Early Years and the Disability Discrimination Act 1995: What Providers Need to Know, National Children's Bureau 2002 – http://www.ncb.org.uk/

Building for Sure Start: Integrated provision for under fives. DfES Sure Start CABE 2004 – http://www.surestart.gov.uk/publicationsandresources/

Most very young children (0-5 year olds) with SEN and disabilities can be included in the whole range of local community settings, from children's centres to nursery classes (3-4 year olds) at a primary mainstream school. A small minority attend special schools. Additional support is provided for them using multi-agency services to meet the child's needs and support the family. Early years provision is not always in purpose built accommodation, so buildings may need to be adapted to provide accessible, child-friendly facilities.

Early years learning

Learning through play is especially important at this age and children with SEN and disabilities take part in a range of play-based communication-rich experiences. If they have a higher level of need, greater support can be provided by more staff.

Environments for very young children need not only to be appropriate for their care and support, allowing space for circulation and for specialist staff using bulky equipment, but also spacious enough to allow different layouts for a variety of activities, toys and play equipment.

Play spaces should be flexible spaces with good visual and physical connections to outdoors.

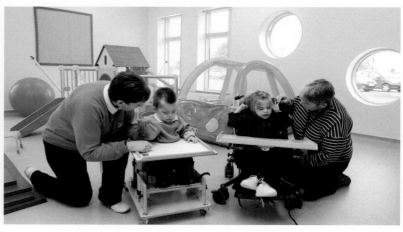

Typical early years spaces

The exact accommodation will depend on the setting and the type of childcare offered – part– or full-time sessions, for example. Nurseries attached to schools may share facilities such as the kitchen and hall but usually have separate entrances, toilets, support spaces and outdoor play areas. There needs to be enough flexibility to support diverse and fluctuating needs.

The typical range of learning and social spaces comprises:

- one or more play spaces
(See Table 3.)

- a small quiet room for 1:1 support

- a covered outdoor play space

- an outdoor area providing a range of experiences

These are supported by:

- storage for belongings, resources and play equipment, and confidential records

- storage for buggies and mobility equipment close to the main entrance

- staff spaces

- a parents' room

- a gated kitchen and laundry nearby

- direct access to toilets and changing rooms

Table 3: Play space - early years

Indoor play areas – statutory

Under 2	3.5 m² per child
2 years old	2.5 m² per child
3–5 years old	2.3 m² per child

Minimum as basis for registration, Early Years Foundation Stage 2008[3]

All areas are for play space only, excluding support, staff, storage etc.

Mainstream schools – guidance

Nursery	63–70 m²

Area given in BB99: 'Briefing Framework for Primary School Projects' for 26 children

Special schools/classes – guidance

Nursery	65–75 m²

Typical space to support about 6-8 children.

3. Refer to: http://www.standards. dfes.gov.uk/eyfs/

C

A covered area directly outside the play space provides children with a broader range of activities and experience.

Inclusive early years provision

The guiding principles of inclusive design for schools set out earlier also apply to early years, with some additional factors:

- Health and safety considerations are particularly important for very young children with SEN and disabilities (for example hygienic sand and water play facilities).

- Ground floor accommodation allows safe, level, easy access to the outdoors, preferably reached directly from indoor play areas.

- While children in early years settings often eat their meals in the main play area, some children need a more sheltered place and support.

- Signage, vision panels and door handles (where appropriate) need to be low enough for young children to reach.

- Ramps should have very shallow gradients to suit very young children using wheelchairs or mobility aids.

- Changes of level may pose risks for some children, so suitable safeguards such as gates, lower level handrails and guardings should be provided.

Support spaces

The following facilities may be provided to support inclusion:

- A sensory space
- A soft play space
- An addtional quiet room or semi-enclosed space for support or therapy
- Storage for mobility equipment
- Battery charging for wheelchairs
- A medical room

Specialist spaces can support inclusion.

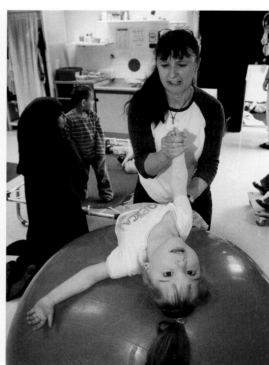

7 Learning and social spaces – primary

Transition from early years to primary is a time of considerable change, especially for those with SEN and disabilities, who often need additional support.

Generally, mainstream primary school spaces can meet the needs of most children with SEN and disabilities but in some cases additional facilities will be needed. These are outlined in this section and described in detail in Support spaces on page 106. Special schools are looked at in more detail on page 56.

Primary learning

In primary education, children are grouped in classes in a class base (open plan or semi-enclosed) or classroom (enclosed) and are taught most of the time by their class teacher, with teaching assistants working across the class. The curriculum covers English, mathematics and science

as core subjects, together with art, science, music, design and technology (including food)[4]. Learning activities are wide and varied, ranging from formal class work to imaginative and constructive play and practical activities.

Typical primary learning and social spaces

Primary mainstream and special schools usually provide:

- classrooms (or bases with shared areas) for whole group work

- separate areas for practical activities, such as cooking (although these activities may take place in a class base if large enough and suitably equipped)

- small rooms for individual and small group work

- library/resources space

- larger spaces (likely to be used by the school and wider community out of school hours) for activities such as drama and movement and physical education, dining and assemblies

- a range of easily accessible outdoor spaces (a useful learning and teaching environment and invaluable for recreational, social, extended school and community use)

These are supported by:

- staff rooms (See page 117.)

- storage (See page 121.)

- toilet and changing rooms (See page 125.)

- kitchen facilities (See page 134.)

Being able to separate noisy and quiet, wet and dry activities easily will help to meet children's diverse needs.

4. For more information on the primary curriculum, refer to: http://curriculum.qca.org.uk/

C

5. Areas taken from Building Bulletin 99: Briefing Framework for Primary Schools 2006 – http://www.teachernet.gov.uk/sbareaguidelines/

Inclusive primary mainstream schools

The guiding principles of inclusive design for schools, page 24, apply to all primary schools. Building Bulletin 99: Briefing Framework for Primary Schools 2006 provides guidance on spaces in mainstream primary schools. The information below focuses on accommodating children with SEN and disabilities.

Primary mainstream class bases

BB99 recommends three sizes of classroom for primary mainstream schools – the usual is for a combination of standard and large-sized rooms.

Small class bases are no longer recommended for new builds, unless they are supplemented by shared teaching area adjacent (e.g. for practical activities). In an existing mainstream school, however, it is possible to achieve an inclusive environment if, for example:

• coats, bags and/or resources can be stored nearby (if relevant)

• fixed furniture can be minimised so staff can re-arrange it as needed

• class numbers can be reduced to accommodate a child using a wheelchair or mobility aids[6]

Standard class bases are large enough for all curricular activities, accommodating one child using mobility aids and a wheelchair, with access to some or all of the space, depending on the layout.

Large class bases enable full accessibility, including for one or more children using mobility aids and/or wheelchairs. They may also be suitable as a class base in resourced provision for children with physical difficulties.

6. It is important to note that smaller groupings might increase the overall number of spaces, staff and staff accommodation.

Table 4: Area guidelines[5] – primary mainstream	
	Area m^2
Small classrooms (30)	Up to 56
Standard classrooms (30)	56 – 63
Large classrooms (30)	63 – 70
Small group rooms (<6)	9 – 12
Library resource (depends on school size)	19 – 54
Food bay/room (15)	35 – 39
Science/design & technology room (15)	35 – 39
ICT room (15)	35 – 39
Music/drama studio (30)	50 – 80
Main hall (depends on school size)	140–200

NB A child with learning aids and a teaching assistant may need the same space as two non-disabled children.

A child using a wheelchair and/or mobility aids may need the space used by three non-disabled children.

If a school has a high proportion (30 to 50 per cent) of children with SEN and disabilities, or a significant number using wheelchairs, access can be improved by having one or two large class bases for each key stage in one or two-form entry mainstream primary schools (i.e. that have one or two new classes of 30 each year), and one large class base for each year in three-form entry mainstream primary schools.

See Furniture, fittings and equipment (FF&E), page 160, for detailed specification.

Floor plans of accessible mainstream class bases

Typical room layouts of accessible class bases, showing:

- space at the entrance and to access key facilities including the whiteboard, resource and practical zones
- direct access to the outdoors, providing an alternative learning environment
- space for a teacher using a wheelchair

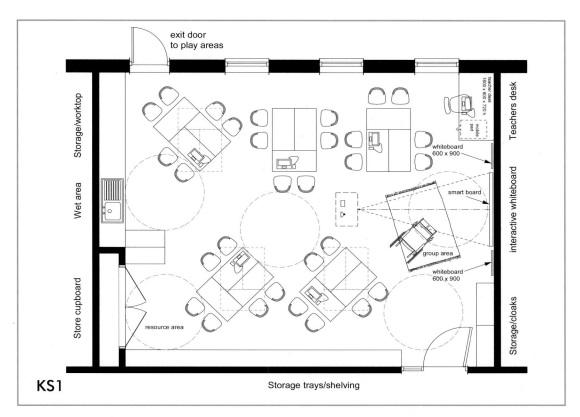

KS1

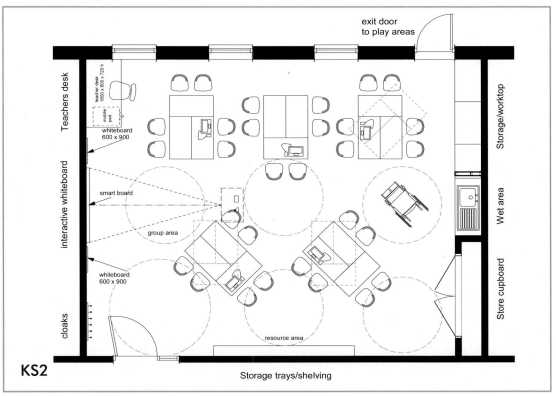

KS2

Some children use special equipment and need additional learning support.

Primary inclusion – key design points

• Classrooms or class bases (which may open onto a shared area) that allow flexibility in learning and teaching

• Easy access to quiet small-group rooms (not accessed from other classrooms, which causes disruption and disturbance)

• The ability for large open plan areas to revert easily to cellular spaces, if need be

• Access from circulation spaces, not other classrooms (which causes disruption and disturbance)

• The potential for arranging different groupings and activities (for example, sitting in a circle, around a table or for individual work) and for zoning activities and separating noisy and quiet

• Links to a variety of outdoor spaces – peaceful quite places as well as noisy active places

• Support spaces and equipment to suit the children at the school

Shared open plan areas can accommodate small groups as needs arise.

Group rooms can be used most flexibly if they open off a shared circulation space.

Primary mainstream support facilities

There is usually enough suitable space in mainstream primary schools to support children with SEN and disabilities but sometimes additional provision is needed to ensure inclusion – for example, extra small group rooms where teachers or visiting professionals can work with children individually[7].

Positioning one small group room so that it can be shared (or used in a variety of ways) offers greater flexibility than having dedicated rooms accessible only from one classroom.

Where there is a greater level of need across a primary school, a whole range of support spaces may be required. Some primary schools may have specialist SEN spaces (such as a speech and language therapy room) to support a particular need. Additional space may be needed for making and storing resources for supporting children with visual impairment – such as large print books, embossing, and specialist ICT.

Typically, the total area required for SEN support facilities may be 75–150m².

The information in Support spaces (page 106) can be used as a guide, although in some cases a reduction in area may be appropriate, depending on need.

Supplementary area may be needed to provide resourced provision or a designated unit.

7. Building Bulletin 99: Briefing Framework for Primary School Projects (2006) lists the following that need to be allowed for in an inclusive mainstream primary school: multi-purpose small group rooms; a medical and therapy room for peripatetic staff and health professionals; an interview room for parents; accessible toilets and hygiene facilities; storage space for educational and mobility equipment and classrooms large enough to allow movement for disabled pupils. The recommended total net area includes a 'float', which can be used to provide extra space. Where there is a significant number of children with SEN and disabilities, an overall area greater than in Building Bulletin 99 may be required – http://www.teachernet.gov.uk/sbareaguidelines/

C

Individual support can take place in the classroom or in an enclosed resourced space.

Typical spaces in a resourced provision include: a flexible class base, small group rooms and dedicated outdoor area.

Resourced provision for SEN

Resourced provision in a mainstream primary school caters for a small number of children who spend varying amounts of time in the mainstream class but need the additional support of a base. (See Special educational provision, page 11.)

Table 5: Typical resourced provision – primary	
Space (group size)	Area m²
Class base 6–12 (typically 8)	50–65
Small-group room	9–12
Staff office	9–12
Storage	4 – 6
Plus specialist support spaces to suit needs	

Depending on numbers, there may be one class base and two small rooms for each key stage. Table 5 gives typical room sizes.

There will also be:

• storage for resources, and mobility equipment (See Storage, page 121.)

• support spaces for children's particular SEN, such as therapy rooms and accessible toilets (See Support spaces, page 106.)

Depending on need, the total supplementary area for resourced provision may be 110–250m².

Resourced provision – primary mainstream

A generic plan for resourced provision in a mainstream primary school. It provides two class bases/ support spaces for around eight children; a medium-sized group room for role play/discussion; a small group room for small group/one-to-one support; a specialist speech and language/sensory therapy room and an office. A similar arrangement could be provided for a range of needs, possibly supplemented by other specialist support spaces such as a VI resources room.
(See Medical, therapy and other support, page 106.)

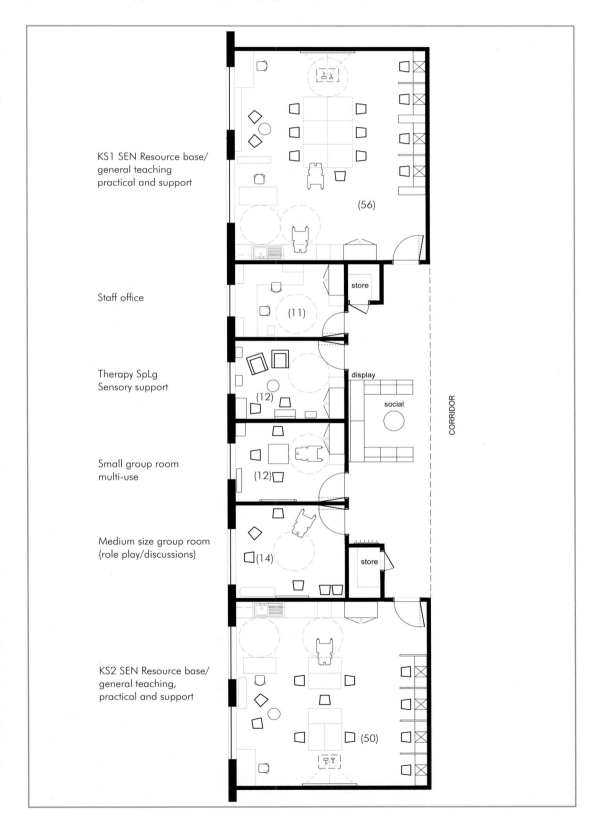

KS1 SEN Resource base/ general teaching practical and support

(56)

Staff office

store

(11)

Therapy SpLg Sensory support

display

(12)

social

CORRIDOR

Small group room multi-use

(12)

Medium size group room (role play/discussions)

(14)

store

KS2 SEN Resource base/ general teaching, practical and support

(50)

C

Designated unit for SEN

Some primary age children with SEN and disabilities need more support and spend most of their time in a designated unit, where they learn strategies to help them access the curriculum in mainstream classes. They may be included in the mainstream school for some social and curricular activities, depending on their individual needs.

The unit typically supports between 10 and 16 children with a particular SEN (although this can vary significantly locally). Typical accommodation may comprise:

• one class base per key stage for timetabled use with children in small groups of up to 8–10, for a full range of curricular and support activities

• two small-group/quiet rooms per key stage – smaller room(s) for individuals or very small groups, larger room(s) for bigger groups, role play and activity

• specialist space(s) relating to children's specific SEN, such as for learning aids and preparation, storage of resources, and mobility equipment

• space(s) for practical work

• support, social and staff space(s)

Depending on numbers and range of need, the total area for a designated unit may be 200–400m².

Table 6: Typical designated unit – primary	
Space (group size)	Area m²
Class base (8–10)	50–65
Small-group room	9–16
Practical base – food	16–20
Social skills base	20–30
Practical base – design and technology, art, science	16–20
Drama	20–30
Children's toilets/coats	12–16
Staff rest room	9–12
Staff toilets	4 – 8
Staff office	9–12
Store – practical base	1 – 2
Store – office records	1 – 3
Store – practical room	2 – 4
Staff office	9–12
Storage for resources	4 – 6

Plus specialist support and resources for particular SEN and disabilities e.g. hygiene room, therapy room. The upper range allows more area for wheelchair users. Where numbers increase towards the size of a small special school, the schedules of accommodation for a special school can be used to ensure adequate and suitable accommodation.

A typical range of spaces in a primary designated unit includes a whole class base and one or more small rooms for one-to-one/small group work.

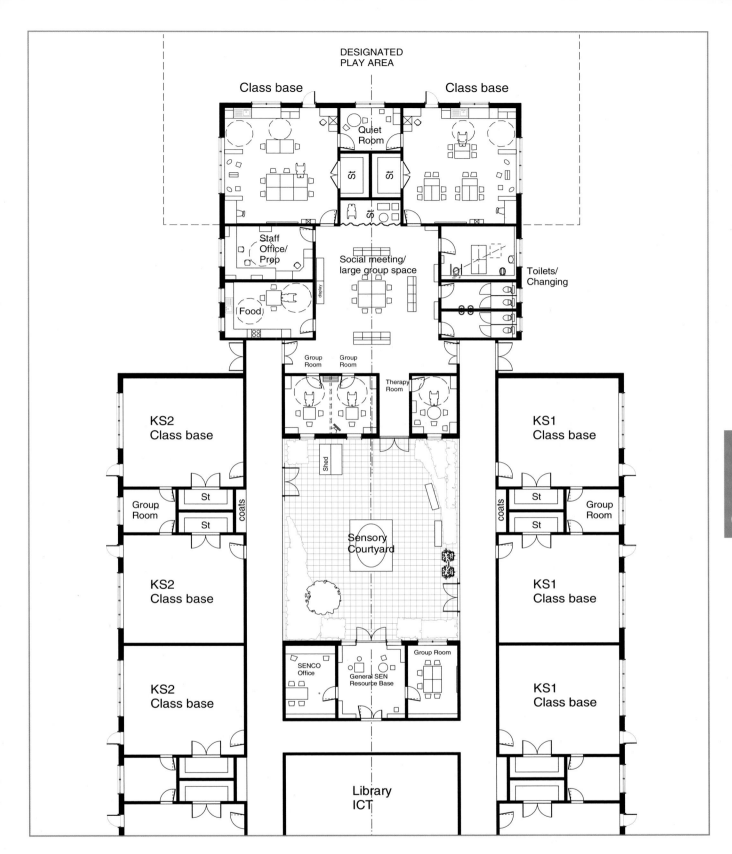

DESIGNATED PLAY AREA

Class base

Class base

Quiet Room

St · St

St

Staff Office/ Prep

Social meeting/ large group space

Toilets/ Changing

Food

Group Room · Group Room

Therapy Room

KS2 Class base

KS1 Class base

Group Room

coats · St · St

Shed

St · St · coats

Group Room

Sensory Courtyard

KS2 Class base

KS1 Class base

SENCO Office

General SEN Resource Base

Group Room

KS2 Class base

KS1 Class base

Library ICT

C

Designated unit – primary mainstream

A self-contained unit closely linked to the rest of the school. It provides two classrooms (KS1 and KS2), a food practical space and two group rooms around a shared multi-purpose space. Points to note:

- Children have access to a sensory garden in a sheltered courtyard.
- The school is also supported by a SEN resource base, SENCo office and group room.
- One group room is shared between the two classrooms. The second is reached from a circulation area and can be divided into two smaller spaces.
- The central area can be used flexibly for learning and social activities.

Primary special schools

Spaces for primary special schools are broadly similar to those for mainstream but with certain additional considerations. In particular, more space is needed because of the higher proportion of children using learning aids and mobility equipment, and the greater number of staff to support them.

As well as the typical spectrum of primary spaces, various medical, therapy and support spaces are needed for the children's specific SEN and disabilities. (See Support spaces, page 106.)

Primary special classrooms/bases

Because of the high level of support they require, children with severe and complex needs are usually taught in small groups or one to one in a class base, by one teacher with teaching assistants and frequently a number of additional support workers.

Flexibility is key to accommodating a variety of activities and meeting a range of needs. For example, some children benefit from working in their own bays. Some children have special chairs.

Classrooms or bases in special schools are laid out and equipped for primary curricular activities, differentiated for the range of need.

Table 7 gives guideline areas for primary classrooms for typical ranges of need but final areas must be based on the number of children and staff, and the range of children's SEN and disabilities catered for in the space.

Table 7: Classrooms – primary special		
Typical range of needs	Number of children	Area m²
A. BESD		
Early years/Reception	6–8	65
KS1 and KS2	6–8	52
B. MLD/SLD/SLCN/ASD		
Early years/Reception	8–10	65
KS1 and KS2	8–10	60
C. MLD/SLD/SLCN/ASD/under 50% PMLD		
Early years/Reception	6–8	70
KS1 and KS2	6–8	60
D. MLD/SLD/SLCN/ASD over 50% PMLD		
Early years/Reception	6–8	75
KS1 and KS2	6–8	65

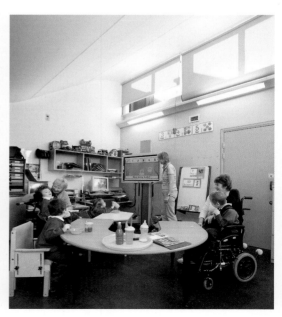

Key Stage 2 class base - primary special

A typical class base (65m²) for six to eight children with a broad range of needs (including SLD and PMLD). The room is flexibly arranged with loose furniture to allow for a range of settings to be created. This layout shows:

- a sensory corner, which can be set up on a temporary basis
- a quiet corner where a child can rest or calm down
- computer workstations, some with screening for children who need additional privacy

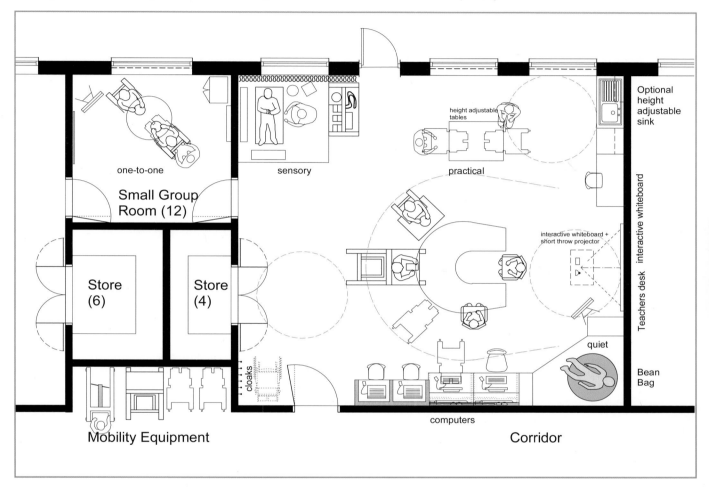

Practical areas

In primary special schools, children have an entitlement to be taught a full range of practical subjects – art, science, food technology and design and technology – either one to one, in small groups or by joining groups together[8]. There may typically be one adult and one assistant for a small group of between two and four pupils.

Practical activities may take place in the classroom (which could affect the floor area), in shared areas adjacent, in specialist bays or rooms, or in large group rooms or other spaces, depending on the school and the children's needs. A small practical space, for instance, might not be large enough for children in wheelchairs. A store for resources will be needed close by.

8. For more information on inclusion in the National Curriculum, refer to: http:// curriculum.qca.org.uk/ key-stages-1-and-2/ inclusion/

Practical areas in open plan spaces need to be easily identified and sited so as not to impede circulation, distract children, or enable them to wander away. Provision will need to be made for the delivery, use and safe storage of tools, equipment and materials.

It is recommended that there are two practical spaces: one for art, science, design and technology, and one for food technology. (Table 8 shows suggested areas.)

All-age schools

In some all-age special schools, primary age children use the secondary specialist spaces.

Table 8: Typical practical spaces – primary special

Space	Area m^2
Food room	25
Food store	2–3
Art, science D&T room	25
Art, science D&T store	3–4

Practical activities can take place in the classroom if it is large enough and activities are suitably zoned.

Art, science, design and technology

A typical practical bay or space for art, science, design and technology needs to be able to accommodate a variety of activities and will typically comprise:

• low-level work tables or benches for small children, a worktop for the teacher, some storage units for equipment and tools, a sink

• one or more height adjustable work tables and sinks

• space for storage, trolley and trays

• a safe and hygienic room layout incorporating outcomes from health and safety risk assessments

• floor and wall finishes for wet and dry activities

Access to suitable outdoor spaces enables children to work with sensory planting or vegetable gardens, to study nature trails or pond life.

Food technology

A separate food space is equipped for demonstrations by the teacher and hands-on activities for children, with:

• worktops (standard height for demonstration by the teacher, low level for small children, including at least a section of adjustable height)

• high and low-level storage units and cupboards.

• a sink (adjustable height)

• a mini-oven, or hob on wheels

• a fridge

In some situations (for example in a school for children with BESD), a social skills training base may be provided next to the food technology space, equipped with typical family living room furniture.

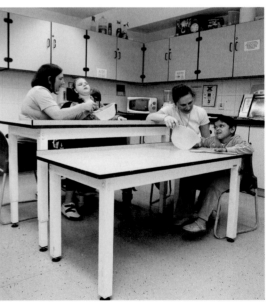

Some schools have a dedicated practical space. Adjustable tables allow for children's different needs.

Performing arts – music, movement and drama

Music teaching may be delivered in a traditional way, similar to mainstream schools, using musical instruments, keyboards and electronic music, or significantly modified to enable children to access their curriculum (and so may require plenty of space).

Sound beam or resonance boards, computer-based sound and light systems may be used in conjunction with physiotherapy, movement and drama. Music therapy may also be provided for children with severe or complex needs to develop their interaction and self-expression.

With suitable acoustic treatment, a range of spaces may be used, depending on local circumstances. The most typical is a specialist music/drama teaching and/or therapy space of 55–65m², which will accommodate most activities for small groups or a class group together.

A smaller room of 15–20m² is useful for one-to-one therapy, with equipment such as a keyboard and some limited space for a child to move.

In some schools a larger group room/music/performance studio (70–80m²) may be provided. (See Table 9.)

Table 9: Typical performing arts spaces - primary special	
Space	Area m²
Small music room	15–20
Store	4 – 6
Music and drama	55–65
Store	6 – 8
Large group room	70–80
Store	6 – 8

A minimally furnished space allows for a number of activities including music therapy.

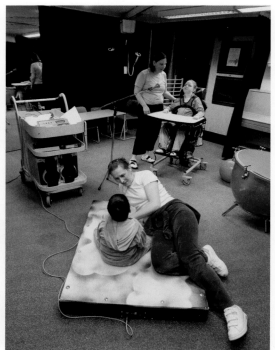

Effective sound insulation, to avoid disturbance and distraction, can be achieved by positioning spaces carefully. If sliding folding doors are used, they should be of the highest acoustic quality. (See Secondary performing arts, page 92, for further detail.)

A store (8m²) should be provided for equipment and props, with suitable security for different users. Dry changing space may also be needed for drama. (See Changing rooms, page 132.)

Flexible use of space

• Positioning a music/drama studio next to a hall, with a sliding folding partition between, gives a choice of three sizes of space, increasing flexibility.

• In an all-age school, a small hall equipped for music, movement and drama could be timetabled for use by all ages, if suitably furnished and equipped.

• A co-located primary special school with a music/drama studio and a hall for assembly and movement (e.g. 100m²) may also have access to the larger mainstream school hall for large gatherings and performances.

The main school hall is often used for a large performance or as an activity space.

C

Learning resource spaces

Learning resource spaces are useful for cross-curricular work and individual support.

Table 10: Typical learning resources – primary special	
Space	Area m²
Small-group room	9–16
Library	15–20
ICT	15–20
SEN resource base	30
Library store	3–4
ICT file server/store	3–6

Small-group rooms

Small-group (or quiet) rooms are an invaluable resource in a primary special school, where they are likely to be used for working with one child or a small group of children with two adults.

An area of 9–12m² is suitable for small groups of ambulant children or one-to-one working with a child who uses a wheelchair. An area of 12–16m² will be needed for two or more wheelchair users.

A group room positioned between two classrooms/bases allows flexible use by each class but it is important that adjacent groups are not disrupted. Providing another entrance from the corridor can add to the flexibility but too many doors into a small room can reduce usable space. A group room sited away from the class may be useful for visiting professionals and for managing behaviour to avoid disturbing another class.

Having an external wall, with windows providing natural light, ventilation and a view out, but without external access, is preferable.

Library

A well-designed library can enhance learning. Children may use computers along with other access technology there, such as Braille readers, touch screens, audio visual or video display and learning resource packs, with toys and reference objects. Shelves and search systems should be at an appropriate height for access by younger children and wheelchair users.

The learning environment should be comfortable and there may be informal seating, such as bean bags.

If the library opens onto a circulation area, it must be sited to avoid disruption since some children with SEN can be disturbed or distracted easily. As with all open plan spaces, security, fire and acoustics issues will also need to be resolved.

A medium-sized group room allows for small groups and local resources (a). Furniture can be used to create different zones of the library (b).

a

b

ICT [9]

ICT is used throughout the school. There may also be a dedicated facility, which may be combined with the library space.

Children with SEN and disabilities use a wide range of equipment, such as interactive whiteboards and/or plasma screens, computers, touch screens, adapted keyboards and access technology, or switching equipment, along with associated software. If there is a dedicated ICT space (15–20m²) for small groups or one to one, it should have easy access and enough room for circulation. If it is a bay, issues of equipment security, visual, noise and movement distraction will need to be resolved. (See also Sensory spaces, page 112 and Information and communication systems, page 167.) Expert advice should be sought on integrated technologies.

SEN resource base

Some schools may have a specialist resource base of around 30m² which is timetabled for small groups of three or four children – for example, to provide extra support for children with ASD.

9. Refer to:
Becta guidance for schools on technical specifications and framework documents at www.becta.org.uk

ICT is used in all areas. Some children have special equipment.

C

Halls and dining

Primary special schools generally have two large spaces, often provided as:

• a multi-functional space of 100–120m² for PE, assembly and large performances

and

• a dining room of 80–120m² (depending on pupil numbers)

A multi-functional hall must be carefully designed to avoid conflict between assembly, performance and SEN needs. It is useful to consider the whole school day, balancing the need to change between functions without wasting time moving equipment and furniture (bearing in mind that some schools assemble in the hall at the end of the day before buses arrive for departure).

10. Refer to Sport England design guidance – http://www.sportengland. org/resource_downloads. htm

Designing Space for Sport and Arts, DfEE, Sport England and The Arts Council 2000 – http://www.teachernet. gov.uk/sbdupublications/

Table 11: Sports hall sizes (Sport England)[10]		
w × d × h	Area m²	Activities
10 × 10 × 3.5m	100	Dance/movement
10 × 14 × 4.5m	140	Table tennis/Boccia
10 × 18 × 6.1m	180	Badminton
Store floor area	40 or 10%	

It makes sense to locate the hall centrally at the heart of the school, limiting travel time for all children from their classrooms.

Activities and equipment used will depend on children's needs and abilities.

Assembly

Assembly is an important time, when all children and staff come together as a whole school community, so it is crucial to create an ambience that reflects the school's ethos, public status and community role. The scale, proportions and height should be functional and age appropriate and there should be suitable security for its use after school hours.

PE

Some children with SEN and disabilities are independently active and able to be involved in a range of physical activity and sport. Others with severe and complex needs, including physical disabilities, need more support and specialist activity programmes. For some children, there may be links with music and movement or between floor work and physiotherapy. An uplifting and energising ambience can help interest children in movement and sport.

The minimum recommended space to accommodate PE activities in primary special schools is 100m². A larger

Table 12: Halls - primary special	
Space	Area m²
Multi-function (PE/assembly)	100–120
PE including badminton	180*
Store	10 – 15
*If funding is available, this size may be preferred for community use.	

Planning points

Uniting a hall space of 100m² and a dining space of 80m² may be a flexible arrangement to support breakfast, after-school clubs and community use for sport, or special interest groups.

Alternatively, providing a large group room/studio space of 80m² next to a hall of 100m², with a high quality moveable acoustic partition between the two, provides a range of options. This may particularly benefit some young children with SEN (for example, those with autism) who find large spaces confusing.

space may be needed for a wider range of sporting activities and if there is community use of the space. (Table 11 shows the range of activities that can be accommodated in typical sports hall sizes)

A hall used for PE should ideally open directly onto an external recreation area and have the following characteristics:

• Proportions that are suitable for curricular use and age-appropriate (large sports halls may be uncomfortable for some children)

• Glare-free lighting

• Finishes and fittings with good impact resistance and good visual contrast, with a warm, safe and slip resistant floor (a sprung floor may be desirable for some activities). For technical information on sports floors, refer to Sport England's Floors for Indoor Sports – http://www.sportengland.org/ facilities_guidance.htm

A schedule of equipment to support the full range of activities should be drawn up in consultation with the school and SEN specialists. Some schools may have traditional wall-fixed equipment of climbing bars and ropes. Others may have large moveable soft items

designed for children with particular disabilities.

An equipment store of at least 10m² will be needed. An area of 15–20m² is needed for large items such as trampolines, goals for football and nets. There may be a separate store for chairs. Long shallow stores directly off the hall are practical. (See Storage, page 121 for more details.) Accessible changing rooms - sited near the hall and close to external sport or multi-games spaces for access and good supervision – will also be needed.

Read more about changing areas on page 132.

For external spaces for physical education, see Outdoor spaces, page 68.

See also Secondary schools, page 97, for design aspects to consider.

Lighting and acoustics in a multi-functional hall need to meet a range of needs, including presentations, musical performances and PE.

C

Dining

Dining together can promote a sense of belonging and inclusion. Some children need further assistance with eating, drinking, developing social skills and managing behaviour as part of their curriculum and progress to independence, and they may need to be able to focus in a quiet, sheltered space away from distraction. Most staff help during lunch, and this should be reflected in the space. Some children may have particular dietary requirements or need specially prepared food.

The size of the dining space will depend on whether all children have to sit and eat together at the same time,

or whether there are phased arrangements. Generally, multiple sittings for dining are not practical for most special schools because of the limited time available and the high level of support required. Designers need to consider the following points:

- A space that is too constricted or busy will cause stress for some users.

- There needs to be enough space between tables for children to circulate, including those in wheelchairs.

- Servery counters need to be low enough for children to see the food.

- Some children may need tube feeding - the feed will need to be prepared in hygienic conditions in a medical room or nurse's room and children fed in privacy. (See Support spaces, page 106.)

See Secondary – dining, page 99, for design aspects to consider.

Dining spaces are sometimes used for other activities such as meetings, music or drama if the acoustics and finishes are appropriate.

Table 13: Dining spaces – primary special		
Space	Number	Area m²
Dining (SLD PMLD/ASD)	56–112	80–135
Dining (BESD)	56–112	80–125
Chair store		8 – 12

Some children need help, time and privacy during mealtimes.

All-age schools

In order to provide an appropriate environment for younger children, all-age schools either stagger lunchtime or have two adjacent dining spaces with a sliding folding partition between that can be opened up for other school activities.

A space for dining is located next to a space for PE and assembly, with a sliding folding partition between the two spaces.

Direct access from the dining space to a protected outdoor area can be a valuable addition.

11. Pitches can be all-weather surfaces or grass, provided they are laid out for the playing of team games. If grass, it should be capable of sustaining seven hours a week, per school, during term time. (Rotation allowing grass to recover may be needed.) Refer to: The Education (School Premises) Regulations 1999 – http://www.teachernet.gov.uk/sbregulatoryinformation/

For technical information on all-weather pitches, refer to Sport England's A Guide to the Design, Specification and Construction of Multi Use Games Areas (MUGAs) Including Multi-Sport Synthetic Turf Pitches (STPs) – http://www.sportengland.org/facilities_guidance.htm

Equipment should be chosen to suit the children.

Outdoor spaces

Experiencing the outdoor environment is an important part both of learning and leisure for children with SEN and disabilities, and a clear rationale should be developed so that outdoor spaces enrich learning, teaching and recreation. Outdoor activities at primary special schools can be adventurous and support children's skill-based learning and enjoyment of play.

A range of spaces should be provided, including:

* outdoor PE facilities

* informal social and recreational areas

* habitat and outdoor classroom areas to support the outdoor curriculum, physical and sensory needs, social and independence skills

Outdoor PE facilities

In special schools many children can take part in team games and other activities similar to mainstream schools. Some will join in simplified games for developing throwing, catching and jumping skills.

Outdoor PE facilities typically comprise:

* sports pitches of grass or artificial surfaces[11] (required for children aged 8 and over, see School Premises Regulations)

* hard-surfaced games courts such as multi-games, tennis courts, and skill-practice areas

Provision should be geared towards the children at the school – wheelchair users might find grass pitches more difficult, in which case appropriate 'all weather' surfaces should be considered to ensure they can participate. Although grass pitches are not as useful to some wheelchair users, it is important that the pitches and access to them are designed and constructed so that wheelchair users can make full use of them.

The total area of sports pitches and hard-surfaced games courts must add up to at least the minimum required in the School Premises Regulations. (See Table 14.) The following meet the Regulations and can be used as a guide for initial planning:

For a primary special school for a wide range of needs:

* one grass pitch of 1000–2000m² for various sport or games activities

* one hard court of 700–1400m² for netball, basketball or multi-games

For a primary special school for BESD:

* one grass pitch of 4018–7344m² for medium (82 x 49m) to large (108 x 68m) football pitches, including margins

* one hard court of 700–1400m² for basketball or multi-games

Table 14: Minimum areas for team game playing fields – all schools[12]	
Total number of pupils aged 8 or over	Area m^2
100 or fewer	2500
101 to 200	5000
201 to 300	10000

Where special schools are built on restricted sites that cannot comply with the Regulations, access to the curriculum should be ensured by partnership arrangements with other schools and centres.

Health and safety risk assessments will be necessary to decide on the locations and the surfaces of courts and pitches, and areas must allow for safe run-offs. There should also be adequate space around play equipment and safety surfaces for soft landings.

External stores will be needed for:

- sports and play equipment (about 10m^2)
- smaller maintenance items (about 10–20m^2)

See Storage, page 121.

Informal social and recreational activities

There should be a variety of areas for different types of play and to enable children to make choices and engage in different activities. For instance:

- to run or kick a ball
- for imaginative or adventure play
- social spaces to sit and talk
- quiet places to be alone

Areas with a combination of hard and soft areas might have play equipment (with safety surfaces), fixed seating and other fixed features. Dividing areas by low fencing and gates can bring variety and help with supervision.

It may be necessary to separate boisterous activities from quieter sheltered spaces for more vulnerable children. Some areas should be partially covered.

Providing safe simulations of hazards that children might meet outside school can encourage the development of independence skills.

The type and amount of sensory stimulus and play equipment should be discussed with staff. For example, some children could become fixated on water, but for others it might be a learning tool.

12. Source: The Education (School Premises) Regulations 1999 – http://www.teachernet.gov.uk/sbregulatoryinformation/

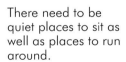

C

There need to be quiet places to sit as well as places to run around.

Habitat and outdoor classroom areas

Classrooms opening directly onto an external area are especially useful for children with SEN and disabilities.

• A covered outdoor space of around 2.5m^2 deep can provide a valuable 'transitional' space between inside and outside.

• An outdoor classroom can be created in 55–65m^2.

Consulting with staff is essential. For instance, direct external access and views over activity might distract some children and access control may be needed. Yet access to a safe contained outdoor place might help other children to calm down. Access via a lobby could help resolve this.

The natural features of any site can provide a rich resource for learning across the curriculum. Grounds can also be enhanced by providing planting, ponds and nature trails, with children and staff involved in their development as part of the curriculum. Effective supervision, appropriate sight lines and security are essential to avoid children straying and to provide protection from unauthorised visitors. The choice of plants is also important.

See Part D, page 142 for more detail on external ramps and steps.

Even small sites can give children access to nature if carefully designed.

Useful guidance on outdoor spaces

• Schools for the Future: Designing School Grounds, DfES, 2006 – http://www.teachernet. gov.uk/sbdupublications/

• Designing for Sport on School Sites – http://www.sportengland.org/facilities_ guidance.htm

• Building Bulletin 99: Briefing Framework for Primary School Projects – http://www. teachernet.gov.uk/sbareaguidelines/

• Standards for School Premises (guide to the Education (School Premises) Regulations 1999) – http://www.teachernet.gov.uk/ sbregulatoryinformation/

• Learning through Landscapes provides advice and guidance - http://www.ltl.org.uk/

Providing shelter from sun and rain increases the usability of outdoor areas.

a

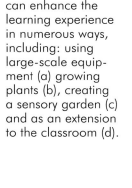

Outdoor spaces can enhance the learning experience in numerous ways, including: using large-scale equipment (a) growing plants (b), creating a sensory garden (c) and as an extension to the classroom (d).

b

c

d

8 Learning and social spaces – secondary

By the time children reach secondary school, their special needs are likely to have been identified and the most suitable provision decided upon. Nevertheless, this is still a significant time of transition for them, and consequently an anxious time for some.

The general provision made in mainstream secondary spaces will be able to meet the needs of some children with SEN and disabilities but additional support facilities will be required in some cases.

Some children benefit from the extra support and stability of resourced provision or a designated unit, with flexible arrangements for them to be included in the main school. Some need the additional support of a special school.

Secondary learning

At secondary level, children progress to a more wide ranging and specialised curriculum, and accommodation can be correspondingly diverse. Rather than spending most of their day in one classroom as they do in primary school, children move around the school to spaces with specialist facilities for different activities.

14–19 year olds often also have vocational training and work experience.

Mainstream schools can be especially large, so some children with SEN and disabilities need assistance when they move between different spaces and to take part in school life.

Typical secondary learning and social spaces

The range of spaces needed will depend on a school's curriculum, size and organisation but will typically provide the following:

- general teaching spaces
- larger spaces for a range of practical specialist and performance subjects
- small rooms for individual and group work
- resource spaces, including library and ICT facilities
- large spaces for physical education and assemblies
- dining and social spaces
- outdoor spaces

These will be supported by:

- staff facilities (See page 117.)
- storage for personal belongings, learning aids and resources (See page 121.)
- accessible toilet and changing rooms (See page 125.)
- kitchen facilities (See page 134.)

Children move around far more in secondary school and it is important that all can travel easily between classrooms.

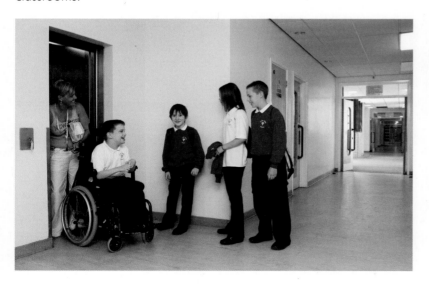

Inclusive secondary mainstream schools

The guiding principles of inclusive design for schools (page 24) also apply to all secondary schools. Building Bulletin 98: Briefing Framework for Secondary School Projects 2004 provides guidance on spaces in mainstream secondary schools. The information below focuses on accommodating children with SEN and disabilities.

Table 15 shows area guidelines from BB98 for the recommended spaces in secondary mainstream schools. In some cases the upper end of the area range may be needed or the space used differently to accommodate the particular needs of the children at the school[13].

13. It is important to note that if group sizes are reduced this might increase the overall number of spaces, staff and staff accommodation needed.

14. Refer to: Building Bulletin 98: Briefing Framework for Secondary School Projects – http://www.teachernet.gov.uk/sbareaguidelines/

Table 15: Area guidelines for secondary mainstream teaching spaces[14]

Space (typical group size)	Zone	Area m²
General teaching		
Small classroom (30)	B	49–56
Standard classroom (30)	C	56–63
Large classroom (30)	D	63–70
Other teaching		
ICT, business studies, language laboratory (30)	E	70–83
Standard art room, science laboratory (30)	F	83–99
Large art room (textiles, 3D) (30)	G	99–115
Electronics and control systems (20)	H	83–100
Food room (20)	I	100–107
Resistant materials, including CAD/CAM (20)	J	107–119
Music classroom (30)	D	63–70

Secondary mainstream spaces – general teaching

Building Bulletin 98 recommends three sizes of general teaching space in secondary mainstream schools:

Small classrooms
(49–56m² for up to 30 children)
If many children have SEN and disabilities or need a high level of support, adjustments will need to be made to how a space of this size is used. For example, class numbers might need to be reduced to allow adequate circulation space for learning aids and teaching assistants. It is not generally recommended to have small general teaching spaces in new school buildings because of their lack of flexibility.

Standard classrooms
(56–63 m² for up to 30 children)
Standard teaching spaces are usually large enough for children with SEN and disabilities to access all relevant curricular activities, allowing for one child using mobility aids and a wheelchair, with access to some or all of the space, depending on the layout.

Large classrooms
(63–70 m² for up to 30 children)
Large teaching spaces are especially suitable for children with SEN and disabilities, since they provide enough room to accommodate one or more children (or staff) using mobility aids and/or wheelchairs, as well as the necessary support staff. They are partic-ularly useful as a base for children with physical difficulties. It is recommended that there is at least one large teaching space for each subject in an average secondary mainstream school (900–1350 pupils) and two or more for each subject in a larger secondary mainstream school (1350–1800 pupils), depending on the children's needs. (Where there are many children with SEN and disabilities, including some with complex needs, a larger space for each subject may be better.)

Secondary mainstream spaces – practical

Practical spaces should be designed to allow all children to take part in the full range of activities. It is important that pupils can access equipment, materials and a suitable workstation/surface to undertake the practical work. The activity and/or the furniture and equipment may need to be adjusted to meet specific needs. A health and safety risk assessment may need to be carried out.

Secondary inclusion – key design points

- Flexible timetabling allows reduction in group size if required.

- Furniture, equipment and servicing positions should allow a range of layouts to meet different needs.

- There should be sufficient space around equipment and machines in practical spaces for those using mobility aids or specialist/adapted equipment.

- Do not underestimate space needed for wheelchair users. A child with a wheelchair and/or mobility aids may need as much space as three non-disabled children. A child with learning aids and a teaching assistant may need the same space as two non-disabled children.

- Consider the impact of scale on some children. If spaces are too large, teaching and supervision may be hampered, some pupils may become confused or distracted, and acoustic treatment and sound-field systems will be needed.

Secondary mainstream 1

An area (63m²) at the top end of the recommended area for a standard general teaching space in Building Bulletin 98, showing access for a wheelchair user. In particular, there is: space at the entrance; an accessible workstation with space for a teaching assistant alongside; space to move to the teacher's table and whiteboard. There is also allowance for a teacher using a wheelchair.

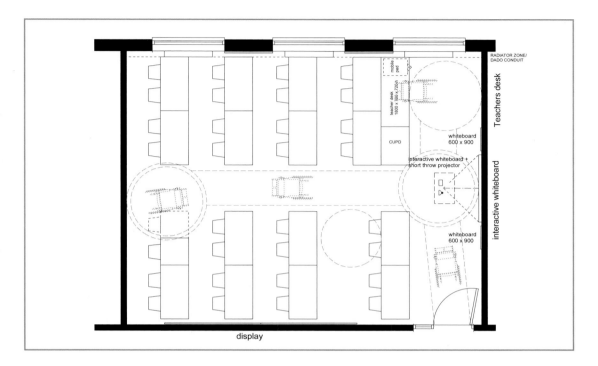

Secondary mainstream 2

A general teaching space in a mainstream school for 18-20 pupils, including a high number of children with disabilities. The area (70m2) is at the high end of the large classroom range in Building Bulletin 98 and allows full accessibility to all parts of the space for pupils and staff using wheelchairs. This demonstrates how a large classroom can be adapted to accommodate a high concentration of wheelchair users.

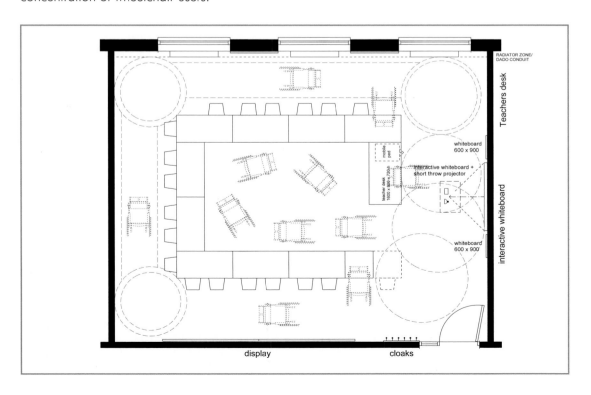

Secondary mainstream science

A mainstream science laboratory for up to 30 pupils. The area (90m²) is in the middle of the recommended area range in Building Bulletin 98 and allows a wheelchair user to access all facilities, including perimeter bench, demonstration bench and whiteboard, ensuring they take part in all activities. A wheelchair accessible table and a height adjustable sink and benching are shown.

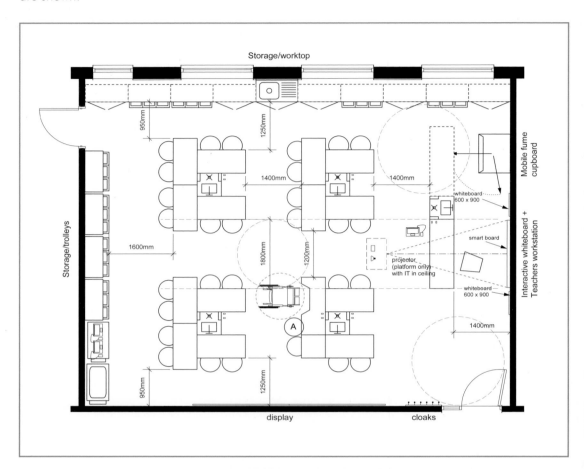

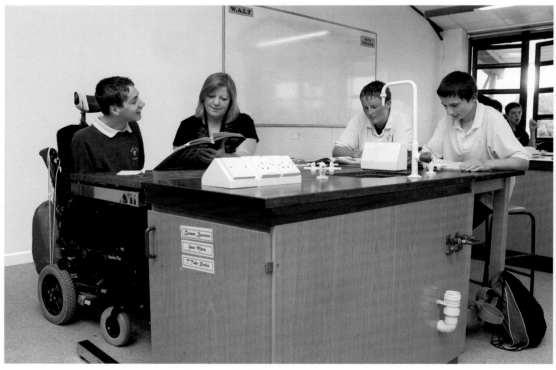

Secondary mainstream support facilities

There is usually enough suitable space in a mainstream secondary school to support children with SEN and disabilities but it may be necessary to provide extra facilities, for example where there is a high number of pupils with additional needs. Building Bulletin 98 recommends providing small group rooms of 9–16 m² for one-to-one support at convenient intervals around the school near staff or departmental offices to support a wide range of needs.

Depending on the numbers of children and range of needs, the total area required for SEN support facilities may be 75–150m².

Some secondary mainstream schools may also have specialist SEN spaces to support a particular need such as a speech and language therapy room. See Support spaces, page 106, for guidance on specialist SEN spaces.

Supplementary area may be needed to provide resourced provision or a designated unit.

Building Bulletin 98: Briefing Framework for Secondary School Projects (2004) lists the following that are allowed for in the recommended gross areas: SEN resource base; multi-purpose small group rooms; office space, medical and therapy rooms for peripatetic staff and health professionals; meeting rooms for parents and carers; accessible toilets and hygiene facilities; storage space for educational and mobility equipment and suitably wide corridors. The recommended total net area includes a 'float', which can be used to provide extra space. Where there is a significant number of children with SEN and disabilities, an overall area greater than in BB98 may be required. Refer to: Building Bulletin 98: Briefing Framework for Secondary School Projects – http://www.teachernet. gov.uk/sbareaguidelines/

C

Mainstream schools may have a specialist SEN resource space for visually impaired children.

Small group rooms should be accessible to wheelchair users.

Resourced provision for SEN

Resourced provision at secondary level caters for a small group of children with a particular SEN or diverse needs, such as physical disability (PD), speech and language difficulty (SLD), moderate learning difficulty (MLD), speech, language and communication needs (SLCN) and hearing impairment (HI). They spend most of their time in mainstream classes but need additional support.

Depending on numbers, there may be one class base and two small rooms for each key stage. Table 16 gives typical room sizes.

There will also be:

• storage for resources, and mobility equipment (See page 122.)

• support spaces for children's particular SEN, such as therapy rooms and accessible toilets (See pages 106 and 125.)

Depending on need, the total supplementary area for resourced provision may be 110–250m².

Typical resourced provision includes a flexible class base zoned for a range of activities, incuding: informal small group work (a), using ICT (b) and whole group work (c).

a

b

c

Table 16: **Typical** resourced provision – secondary	
Space (group size)	Area m²
Classroom (6–12)	50–65
Small-group room	12–20
Therapy/specialist SEN	15–20
Staff office	9–12
Storage	4 – 6
Plus specialist support spaces to suit needs	

Secondary resourced provision

A generic plan for resourced provision in a mainstream secondary school. It provides two general teaching/support spaces for around eight children, two small group rooms and a specialist speech and language therapy room. A similar arrangement could be provided for a range of needs, possibly supplemented by other specialist support spaces such as a VI mobility training space. (See Medical and therapy spaces, page 106.)

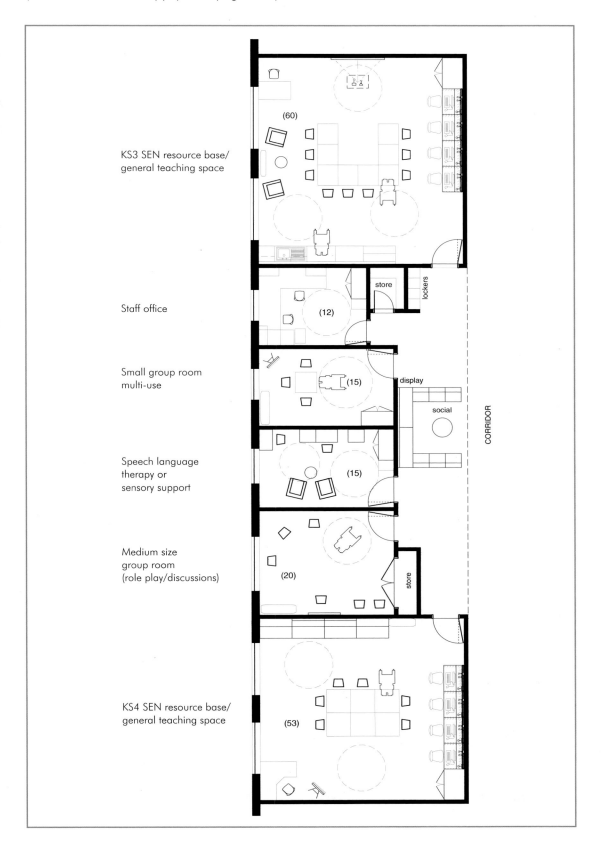

KS3 SEN resource base/general teaching space (60)

Staff office (12)

store

lockers

Small group room multi-use (15)

display

social

CORRIDOR

Speech language therapy or sensory support (15)

Medium size group room (role play/discussions) (20)

store

KS4 SEN resource base/general teaching space (53)

C

Designated unit for SEN

A designated unit at secondary level has similar spaces to resourced provision but with a wider range of teaching spaces, since children spend most of their time there. The extent to which the children use the specialist mainstream spaces, such as science labs, will depend on their particular needs and the suitability of the mainstream facility. The numbers may vary in a designated unit but are usually small, supporting, for example, 10 to16 children with a particular SEN.

Where there is provision for a range of needs, such as hearing impairment (HI), autistic spectrum disorder (ASD), behavioural, emotional and social difficulties (BESD) or speech and language difficulties (SLD), additional teaching spaces may be required to resolve conflicting demands.

Depending on numbers, there may be one or two classrooms, two small rooms and practical spaces, according to need. Specialist SEN spaces, such as a therapy space, may also be required if not already provided within Building Bulletin 98. The total supplementary area for a designated unit may be 220–440m². Table 17 shows a typical range of spaces. See also Support spaces, page 106.

A typical designated unit includes practical spaces as well as general classrooms, for example art/D&T (a) or food technology (b). There may also be an ICT resource area (c).

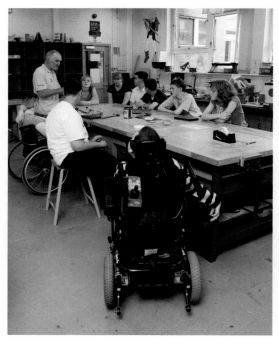

a

Table 17: Typical range of spaces for a designated unit – secondary	
Space (group size)	Area m²
Classroom (8–10)	50–65
Small-group room	12–20
Therapy/SEN specialist	15-20
Practical room - food	50–60
Social skills base	20–30
Practical room – art/D&T	50–60
Practical room – science	50–60
ICT/library resources	25–50
Storage for resources	2 – 6
Toilets/coats	12–16
Storage – social skills base	2 – 4
Storage – office records	2 – 4
Storage – practical room	2 – 6
Staff rest room	9–12
Staff office	9–15
Staff toilets	4 – 8

Plus specialist support and resources for children's needs, e.g. hygiene rooms

The upper range allows more area for wheelchair users.

Where numbers increase towards the size of a small special school, the schedules of accommodation for a special school can be used to ensure adequate and suitable accommodation.

Secondary designated unit

A sample plan for a designated unit for pupils with BESD at a secondary mainstream school. The typical range of spaces includes two general teaching spaces, practical spaces for art and design and technology, food and science, supported by two group rooms and a shared social space. Points to note:

- General teaching room sizes allow for variation in layout, including space between individual tables.
- Each pupil can have their own workspace in the practical rooms.
- The small group rooms can be used for counselling or learning support.
- Direct access to the outside from practical spaces broadens the learning opportunities.
- ICT is provided in all spaces.

b

c

Secondary special schools

The design of a secondary special school should reflect the older age of the children and help to support their progress to independence and participation in the wider community.

See Inclusive design principles for schools, page 24, and Access and circulation, page 38, for the provision that should underpin all school design for children with SEN and disabilities.

In special schools, children are entitled to be taught the same statutory curricular subjects as in mainstream schools, adapted to suit their needs[15]. Since the range of needs may fluctuate over time (as the school population changes and allowing for some needs to be transient), it is particularly important that the accommodation provides enough flexibility and adaptability.

The typical range of learning and teaching spaces must be configured and suitably equipped to meet children's needs. Where needs are diverse and potentially conflicting, additional learning and teaching spaces may be required.

Various medical therapy and support spaces will also be needed. (See page 106.)

15. For more information on secondary age learning, refer to: http://curriculum.qca.org.uk/index.aspx

The size and layout of general teaching spaces varies, depending on need. For example: space between children in a BESD school (a); a U-shaped table arrangement to enable children with hearing impairment to see the teacher and each other signing and lip-reading (b); plenty of space around furniture where some children use wheelchairs or other mobility aids (c).

General teaching spaces

General teaching spaces are used for a variety of activities, including as tutor bases. The area required will depend on children's particular needs. Table18 gives typical area guidelines and group sizes.

Table18: Typical general teaching spaces - secondary special		
Typical range of needs	Number of children	Area m²
A. BESD		
	6 – 8	52
B. MLD/SLD/SLCN/ASD		
	8–10	60
C. MLD/SLD/SLCN/ASD/less than 50% PMLD)		
	6 – 8	60
D. MLD/SLCN/ASD/SLD more than 50% PMLD		
	6 – 8	65

a

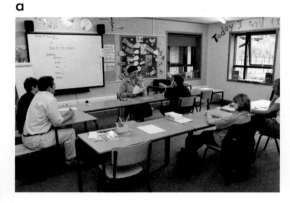

b

c

Secondary special school – general teaching spaces

Two general teaching spaces for groups of six to eight pupils are shown, one of 65m² for pupils with severe and complex SEN and disabilities (a) and the other of 52m² for children with BESD (b). Both spaces have a large walk-in store directly off the classroom, for convenience.

Points to note on the 65m² space:
- The small group room is shared between a pair of classrooms.
- ICT carrels provide individual workstations for concentrated work.
- Loose tables can be arranged to suit needs.
- Wheelchair users can move comfortably around the whole room.
- Some ICT workstations may house equipment specific to one child's needs.
- There is plenty of space around the entrance door and space to 'park' mobility equipment when not in use.
- Mobility equipment and personal belongings are close to the classroom and easy to access.

Points to note on the 52m² space:
- Loose tables are arranged to give each pupil their own space but tables can be rearranged to suit activities and need.
- The small group room can be used for counselling, learning and behaviour support. Opening off the corridor, it can be shared with other classes.

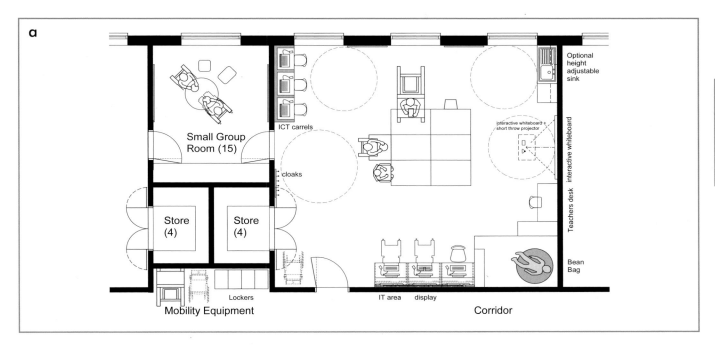

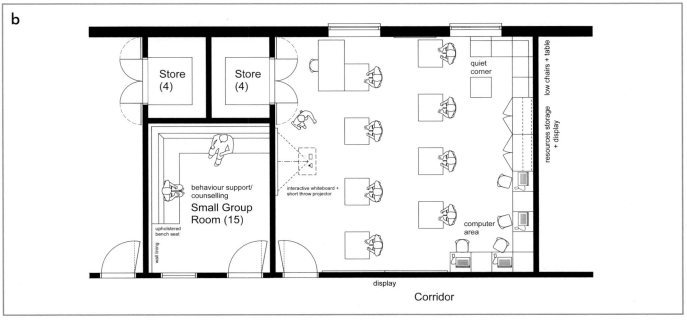

Practical spaces

Children in special schools are entitled to the full range of practical specialist subjects and may be involved in a variety of ways, depending on their special needs and disability. Some children work towards GCSE or equivalent. Others do simple experiments and other practical tasks, as well as a variety of multi-sensory and developmental activities, which could need access to ICT and sensory spaces.

Some children have little independent movement and need access to technology, specialist controls or assistance (for which sufficient space is needed). Children using wheelchairs or other mobility aids need space to move safely around machinery and other children doing practical work, and may need machines and equipment to be adjusted in height for them.

Most special schools require one specialist space for each practical subject, including science, art, design and technology (including food technology). Guidance is given below on each subject. (Table 19 gives area guidelines.)

In some small special schools where there is a higher level of need and a full range of practical specialist subjects is taught one to one or in very small groups, a smaller practical specialist subject space (50–60m2) may be suitable for one teacher, an assistant and a group size of three or four.

In certain circumstances, there may be more than one practical subject in the same space (60–75m2), as long as the activities are compatible and health and safety requirements are met. For example, design and technology and art may share a space. The subject display, resources, furniture, fittings and equipment should be suitably arranged in separate parts of the room for separate timetabled use.

Table 19: Typical practical spaces – secondary special	
Subject	Area m2
Science	60–65
Prep room/store	15
Art	60–65
Art resources store	6 – 9
Kiln room	4 – 6
Art work in progress store	5 – 8
Food technology	60–65
Food store	3 – 6
Food resources store	3 – 6
Design & technology*	65–90
D & T prep/storage (if provided)	20
D & T resources store	7–10
D & T work in progress store	6–9

*including CAD/CAM where provided.

A larger space (75–90m2) may be required for design and technology in some circumstances (see below) or for vocational training, such as catering. (See Learning and social spaces – Post 16, page 104.)

A clear, easily understood, accessible furniture and equipment layout based on the equipment schedule in the brief and children's particular needs is particularly important for practical spaces. Safety is also crucial, with measures including alarm systems, slip-resistant flooring and visual contrast between surfaces to help children move around safely.

For some children with SEN it is important that the space clearly reflects the particular character of the subject being learned. It helps them understand the activities and focus on the task. Furniture layout, display and finishes can all contribute.

Science

A typical science space of 60–65m² is large enough for one teacher, support staff and six to eight children. A preparation room of around 12m² will be needed nearby for storing chemicals[16] and equipment and preparing material for practical work. (See Support section, page 106.)

Where provision is based on a mainstream science laboratory, reference can be made to Building Bulletin 80[17], with modifications depending on children's needs - for example, for children with sensory impairments and/or physical disabilities, including suitable access for wheelchair users[18] (for which specialist advice is required).

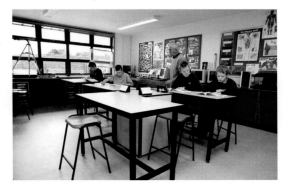

An accessible specialist science laboratory for one teacher, support staff and between six and eight children may have:

• loose standing-height tables, some of which should be height adjustable

• fixed perimeter benching, part of which should be height adjustable, with a height adjustable wash-up sink

• three service hubs that contain gas and power, as appropriate. Some or all of the hubs should be height adjustable for easy access for wheelchair users

• three laboratory sinks, either as part of the service hub or in the perimeter benching. At least one of these may need to be adjustable height, with accessible tap controls, and adequate elbow room and workspace either side

• a fully equipped demonstration bench (as long as the whiteboard is still accessible)

• a fume cupboard, if needed - sited so as not to obscure the views of the teacher and whiteboard

There should be sufficient space for children and staff (including those using wheelchairs) to circulate with ease and to participate in all activities, including gathering around for presentations or demonstrations.

Other possible layouts include peninsular service units forming bays, or fixed units integrating work surface and service hub. The relative merits of these alternatives should be reviewed for the type of SEN and disability, the curriculum delivery, and the supervision and safety requirements.

Safety features of an inclusive laboratory include:

• emergency cut-off points for services, with easy access for staff

• visual as well as auditory alarms

There will also be scientific studies outdoors, so there should be, for example, access to planting, ponds, vegetable garden, greenhouse and nature trails.

There should be room for pupils to gather for a presentation/ demonstration.

Carefully positioned, easily identifiable and operable controls for service outlets may be needed for people with physical or sensory impairments – for example, services and controls can be mounted in a fascia for easy access. For other children, services may be housed integrally in an adjustable height rise and fall drum and concealed as part of the furniture design to ensure services do not cause a distraction, are exposed only when in use and are not easily tampered with when not required.

16. For more information on storing chemicals, refer to: COSHH – http://www.hse.gov.uk/coshh/

17. Building Bulletin 80, Science Accommodation in Secondary Schools – http://www.teachernet.gov.uk//sbdupublications/

18. BS 8300: Design of buildings and their approaches to meet the needs of disabled people, includes guidance on spaces between tables for wheelchair users – http://www.bsi-global.com/shop

C

Design and technology

Generally, a space of 65–70m² will be adequate for design and technology in a special school. If large machinery or specialist equipment is needed for those children working to a mainstream curriculum (for example in a school for children with BESD or HI), the area may need to increase to 90m². There needs to be an adjacent room for the preparation of materials and stores for materials, work in progress and secure storage for substances hazardous to health[19]. See Support spaces, page 106.

A light and airy design workshop provides an atmosphere where children enjoy carrying out practical tasks, helping them acquire skills. Tasks range from simple ones requiring no more than hand tools, card and scissors for model-making, through to those needing specialist equipment or large floor-standing machines such as a lathe.

The notes below, together with reference to Building Bulletin 81[20], can be used as a basis from which to design a space but it is important to discuss with staff how to meet diverse needs. In particular, safeguards need to be made for children who are identified as a risk or as being at risk.

19. Refer to: COSHH – http://www.hse.gov.uk/coshh/

20. Refer to: Building Bulletin 81, Design and Technology Accommodation in Secondary Schools – http://www.teachernet.gov.uk//sbdupublications/

A typical layout for a design and technology space may include:

• an interactive whiteboard with space around for group work

• perimeter benches with bench-mounted machines, storage underneath (provided there is no safety risk) with at least some part being height adjustable

• two sinks housed in the benching (at least one to be adjustable height)

• floor-mounted machinery at the perimeter

• free standing workbenches (including some height adjustable) providing access to a vice for each child

• areas for safe display of children's work to celebrate their achievements

• dust-free areas (possibly a separate space) for ICT/CAD-CAM and design work

• hot-works equipment e.g. a forge (if required), positioned with some degree of separation for health and safety

NB For children with hearing impairment and those who need to see, or be seen by, the teacher, it may be better to arrange machinery to face into the room so that the teacher's instructions and visual alarms are more readily visible. Additional space may be required so that everyone can move around machines safely.

Security and safety measures include the following:

• Emergency cut-off points for electrical services and an emergency stop button at each machine

• Visual and auditory alarm signals, carefully positioned in the space for visibility[21]

• Safe distances around all machines, with appropriate floor markings, taking account of those using wheelchairs and other mobility aids

• Design for active and passive supervision, encouraging positive behaviour (In a setting for children with behavioural difficulties, provision for security of materials and tools is paramount.)

Any harmful particles or fumes must be extracted. Dust extraction is required from some wood working machines and rapid extract ventilation may be required.

Noisy machinery and printers may need some form of acoustic treatment, screening, or shrouding, or be in a separate space.

21. Refer to: BS 4163 Health and safety for design and technology in schools and similar establishments – http://www.bsi-global.com/shop

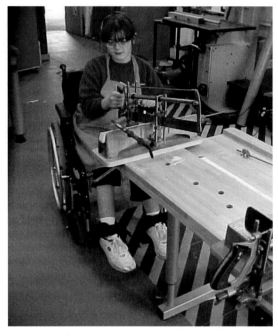

Some children need adapted equipment and/or adjustable furniture to enable them to take part in all activities.

Enough space around machinery is particularly important for children with SEN and disabilities.

Food technology

Specialist food technology spaces should be designed to encourage young people to enjoy food and take an interest in their own health and well-being.

A specially equipped room of 60–65m^2 will be suitable in most situations for up to eight children, with one teacher and one teaching assistant. There should also be stores for food (4m^2) and resources (4m^2).

The room may be laid out in a similar way to a mainstream school. The notes below, together with reference to Building Bulletin 81, can be used as a basis from which to design a layout, subject to detailed discussions with staff on any adaptations and modifications for the type and range of special educational needs. There should be:

• worktop space for each child, with access to a cooker, sink and drainer (generally one between two pupils, but this needs to be checked with the school), some units to be height adjustable

• specially adapted fittings which support life skills and independence training, especially important for young people with visual impairment

• a layout that is appropriate for the children, teaching approach and supervision requirements – for instance, whether cookers and sinks are all around the perimeter or arranged in a series of 'bays'

• clear sightlines and easy access around kitchen units for supervision of young people working alongside each other (There may need to be additional circulation space for clearance between workstations – side to side and back to back – to minimise interference, avoiding positions directly opposite, which could promote conflict.)

• storage units at high or low level and a refrigerator

There may also need to be:

• special fittings with light and/or sound signals for young people with sensory impairment

• a corner space, suitably arranged to support a work space, with low sensory stimulation and minimal distraction

Where life skills are taught, additional equipment may be needed, which should be specified in the brief.

In some situations, for example in a school for children with BESD, a social skills training base or common room may be provided next to the food technology space. See Social skills training, page 116.

There needs to be:

• a hygienic environment

• easy access to emergency cut-out controls for services[22]

• sufficient circulation space for children to work individually (independently or assisted), in pairs or in small groups

22. Refer to: BS 4163 Health and safety for design and technology in schools and similar establishments – http://www.bsi-global. com/shop

Some children need more space around them to avoid conflict.

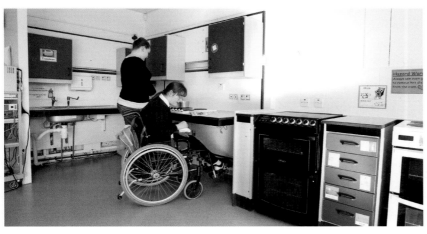

Some children may need adjustable height sinks, hob and worktops so they can take part fully in cooking activities.

Loose tables can be arranged for practical work, group discussions or non-practical work.

C

Art

Secondary special schools should have a fully equipped specialist art room, providing for all aspects of two- and three-dimensional art. It is important to have space that is light and airy, with a relaxed atmosphere and an uplifting and inspiring setting.

Generally, a space of 60–65m^2 is recommended. Stores should be provided for resources (7m^2) and for work in progress (6m^2). (See pages 123–4.)

If a kiln is provided, it needs to be in a separate space. An area of 4-6m^2 is usually adequate, depending on the size of the kiln and provided there is sufficient safe clearance for access by an adult.

Building Bulletin 89[23] can be used as the basis for designing an art room, to be modified to suit the special needs of the pupils. A typical space will have:

- enough sturdy loose tables for the class size – some may have sloping boards and some may need to be height adjustable

- a large layout surface (if required) for group or project work or for textiles or screen printing

- fixed perimeter benching – some may be at different heights, with storage above and below, allowing knee recesses for wheelchair users, as required

- two sinks, one for paints, one with a clay trap, sometimes a third large one for cleaning screens, at least one to be height adjustable, depending on the number of young people with physical difficulties

ICT will be needed in the space or nearby resource area, possibly shared with design and technology. 2D and 3D art display can enhance circulation areas but should not impede visibility and must comply with fire safety requirements.

Access to the outdoors is beneficial for many art activities, including for large-scale making.

Daylight is essential for art activities, with north light traditionally being preferred for its evenness. Some means of control will be needed.
Local rapid extract ventilation may be required – for example, for the use of some glue and sprays – and a risk assessment may be necessary.
There may need to be arrangements for the water service to be isolated (or for the sinks to be covered) if water is a diversion for some children.

NB Visits to museums or galleries will require accessible transport facilities at the school. See Access, arrival and departure, page 38.

23. Art Accommodation in Secondary Schools, available from: http://www.teachernet. gov.uk/ sbdupublications/

Children work in 2D and 3D and in a range of media.

A good level of daylight is particularly important for art.

Performing arts – music, movement and drama

Music, movement and drama activities may be similar to those in secondary mainstream schools or differentiated and adapted to suit diverse needs. The range of activities may include:

- playing small and large traditional or electronic instruments
- storytelling, singing, dancing, drama, acting, movement and performance
- making pop music, developing DJ and sound recording skills
- using interactive ICT in conjunction with multi-sensory work
- sound beam or resonance boards, used in conjunction with physiotherapy, movement and drama

A music/drama room of 65–80m² will support most needs. A clear height of 2.7–3.5m will create a reasonable volume for good sound quality and should be sufficient for simple stage lighting and ceiling-mounted fittings.

A performance studio of 80–120m² may be suitable for a larger school or where there is a relevant specialism. The school hall may also be used. (See page 96.)

An en-suite recording room of 15–20m², accessible to wheelchair users, is an invaluable 'extra' - advice should be obtained from specialist consultants.

Table 20: Typical performing arts spaces – secondary special	
Space	Area m²
Music/drama	65 – 80
Performance studio	80–120
Recording room	15 – 20
Music/drama store	10 – 15

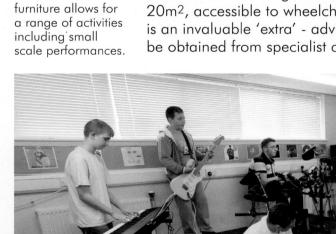

A flexible space with minimal furniture allows for a range of activities including small scale performances.

The music, movement and drama space needs to be a flexible space with loose tables capable of accommodating free-standing instruments such as piano or drums, keyboards with computer interfaces, hand-held instruments, and sound beam or resonance boards. Drama activities may involve the use of props, wardrobe, light and sound equipment and demountable stage units.

The design of the studio space should reflect the subject, using appropriate texture and materials, so creating a setting for inspiring and supportive exploration of music and drama.

There should be full blackout facilities, good quality room acoustics and effective sound insulation.

A range of light and sound equipment may be used.

A sound proofed recording studio may be provided in some schools.

For more information on the detailed design of these spaces, refer to Building Bulletin 86 Music Accommodation in Secondary Schools – http://www.teachernet. gov.uk/sbdupublications/

Theatre lighting and blackout curtains allow a range of envronments to be created

C

Learning resource spaces

Secondary special schools have a range of learning resource spaces.

Table 21: Typical learning resource spaces – secondary special	
Space	Area m^2
Small–group room	12–20
Library	30–60
ICT resource	30–40
ICT (as a specialist subject)	50–60
SEN resource base	30
Library store	3 – 4
ICT file server/store	3 – 6

Small-group rooms

Small-group (or quiet) rooms are an invaluable resource that can be used flexibly by staff for individual and small group work or therapy, as well as by children for calming down. One small-group room shared between two or three classrooms is suitable for most secondary special schools. An area of 12-15m^2 is suitable for small groups of ambulant children or one-to-one working with a child who uses a wheelchair. An area of 15-20m^2 will be needed for two or more wheelchair users.

Library

The library space should be light, airy, quiet, calm and orderly, where books and ICT resources can provide an interactive environment.

• Children will use access technology such as Braille readers, touch screens, audio visual or video display and associated resources.

• Shelves and search systems should be at an appropriate height for everyone, including wheelchair users.

• There are usually loose tables, screened workstations and low seating.

• Blackout or dim-out blinds may be needed for ICT projection.

If the library is open plan, it must be designed to resolve issues of fire, security, distraction and disruption.

ICT

ICT will be used across the school and there may also be small ICT resource areas, possibly linked to the library. Some schools may have a dedicated ICT space timetabled for whole class use and/or as a resource facility.

See Information and communication systems, page 167 for information on room layouts and furniture for ICT.

SEN resource base

Some schools may have a specialist resource base of around 30m^2 which is timetabled for small groups of three or four children - for example, to provide extra support for children with ASD.

Other resource spaces

There may also be small spaces supporting specialist subjects, such as a kiln room for art (see page 90), or a recording room for music (see page 92).

C

Halls and dining

Secondary special schools generally have two large spaces to be used for PE, assembly, performance and dining. These are typically provided as Either:

• a sports hall of around 306m² (17m x 18m) enabling children to participate in a full range of activities, including basketball and five-a-side football

and

• a dining, assembly and performance space of 80–120m²

or:

• a multi-functional space of 140–180m² for PE and movement, assembly and performance

and

• a dining room of 80-120m²

Where a space is used for more than one type of activity, it is important that all curriculum needs are met. It is useful to look at the whole school day, taking account of the time needed to move equipment and furniture and the fact that some schools assemble in the hall at the end of the day before buses arrive for departure. Careful detail design will be needed, for example floor finishes, lighting and acoustics, to ensure functions are not unduly compromised.

Some larger special schools provide (where funding allows) a sports hall of 486m² to broaden the range of sporting activities, especially where there is extensive community use.

Foldaway 'bleacher' seating can be very useful in a multi-functional space but wheelchair access will be restricted.

24. Refer to: Building Bulletin 93 Acoustic Design for Schools – http://www.teachernet.gov.uk//sbdupublications/

Assembly and performance

School assembly is an important time when all children and staff gather together in the school hall as a whole school community.

It makes sense to locate a hall used for assembly and performance centrally, to limit travel time for children from their class base. The following need to be considered:

• A raised stage will restrict disabled access unless a ramp or lift is provided. Foldaway 'bleacher' seating may be flexible and give a good view of the stage but restrict access for wheelchair users.

• Floors should be low glare and if also used for PE/movement, impact-energy absorbing. If a sprung floor is provided, it may need strengthening for the runners for bleacher seating.

• There should be even distribution of light. Side lighting at high level is preferred, as end glazing produces glare. Curtains or blinds will be needed for full blackout facilities (but they must not hamper opening windows or restrict ventilation). Some stage lighting may need to be provided for performance but any lighting bars or grids will need to be at 6m clear height if the space is used for sport.

• Acoustics are particularly important in a multi-functional space. Sound equipment should be provided for performance. Sound-field systems and induction loops may need to be installed. The space should have effective sound separation and insulation with good quality room acoustics[24].

• Means of escape are a particular issue. (See Fire safety and evacuation, page 158.)

PE[25]

Physical education (PE) for children with SEN and disabilities particularly encourages awareness of body and space and improves manipulative development, mobility and activity skills which, along with social and teamwork skills, can nurture progress to independence. An uplifting and energising atmosphere can encourage children to take part and be actively involved in movement and sport. Some children who are not physically disabled may have a high need for activity and can take part in a range of sports. Others may be involved in adapted – including wheelchair – sports. Those with severe and complex needs, including physical disabilities, need more support and specialist activity programmes.

A hall used for PE should, where possible, open onto an external recreation area and have the following characteristics:

• Wall, floor and ceiling finishes should be selected to balance the practical need for durability, impact resistance and protection from projectiles, with the need for appropriate ambience and acoustics.

• To avoid injury, walls should be strong and smooth, with no projections.

• Floors should be low glare and impact-energy absorbing. A sprung floor may be needed (and can be suitable for children with hearing impairment). Floor markings may be required. For technical information on

sports floors, refer to Sport England's Floors for Indoor Sports – http://www.sportengland.org/ facilities_guidance.htm

All-age schools

A hall equipped for secondary PE and sport may also be available for primary PE (with appropriately sized equipment), or for large gatherings.

A multi-functional space can be used for assembly, performance and PE if it is suitably equipped and has suitable lighting and acoustic qualities.

25. Refer to: Designing for Sport on School Sites, Sport England 2007 which also provides links to useful guidance on sports facilities – http:// www.sportengland.org/ resource_downloads.htm and Inspirational Design for PE and School Sport – http://www.teachernet. gov.uk/sbdupublications/

Some schools may have a larger PE space for a range of sporting activities.

C

26. Refer to: Designing Space for Sport and Arts, DfEE, Sport England and The Arts Council 2000. http://www.teachernet. gov.uk/sbdupublications/

Table 22: Halls – secondary special[26]			
Space	Area m²	Height (m)	Activities
Multi-function (PE/assembly)	140	4.5	Dance, movement, table tennis
Multi-function (PE/assembly)	180*	6.1	Badminton, keep fit
Sports hall	306	6.1-7.6	5-a-side football, mini basketball
* Preferred for community use by Sport England			

- Wall-hung fold-out equipment will need to be recessed and concealed behind flush door panels.

- If specialist wheelchair sports are to be included, a clear opening of 1100mm to doors is recommended by Sport England to be wide enough for specialist sports wheelchairs[27].

- Lighting for sport may also be required – for example, lighting of 300–400 lux with ceiling-mounted fittings either side of badminton court lines.

Table 22, page 97, shows the range of activities that can be accommodated in typical sports hall sizes.

Some schools may have traditional wall-fixed equipment of climbing bars and ropes. Others may have large moveable soft items designed for children with particular disabilities. A schedule of equipment to support the full range of activities should be drawn up in consultation with the school and SEN specialists.

An equipment store of at least 15m^2 will be needed. An area of 20–30m^2 is needed for large items such as trampolines, goals for football, and nets. Long shallow stores directly off the hall are often preferred. If wheelchair sports are to be played, it is important that convenient and secure storage is allowed for the sports chairs. Further information on designing for sports chairs can be found in Sport England's technical guidance note, Accessibe Sports Facilities. Accessible changing rooms – positioned near the hall and close to external sport or multi-games spaces for ease of access – are essential.

Read more about changing areas on page 132. For external spaces for physical education, see Outdoor PE facilities, page 101.

27. Refer to: the Sport England publication, Accessible Sports Facilities 2008 – http://www.sportengland.org/resource_downloads.htm

28. Refer to: Building Bulletin 93 Acoustic Design for Schools – http://www.teachernet.gov.uk//sbdupublications/

Community use

Where halls are also used by the community, the following points should be considered:

- Additional separate toilet and changing facilities and more storage may be needed.

- Access to refreshment facilities is useful.

- Access to all facilities will need to be controlled so that community users do not need to enter the rest of the school – zoned planning will facilitate this.

- A ceiling height of 6.1–7.6m may be preferred for some sports (e.g. badminton) – but this may conflict with acoustic requirements, since some children with SEN and disabilities may find large volumes and noise disorientating or confusing[28].

Dining

General points are made in Primary special schools – dining, page 66. In secondary schools, there are likely to be self-service arrangements for dining, as children progress towards greater independence. Table 23 shows area guidelines. In particular, there needs to be:

- a suitable arrangement for queuing and paying systems

- a semi-screened area with subdued colours, offering some privacy and quiet, without distraction, helping pupils who need to focus on their eating

- seating layouts that support the chosen dining style and children's needs (e.g. adjustable height furniture)

- sufficient flexibility to allow for changing needs, avoiding fixed furniture

A dining space may also be used for music and drama activities if the acoustics and finishes are suitable.

Table 23: Typical dining spaces – secondary special

Range of need	Number	Area m²
SLD/PMLD/ASD	64–96	100–120
BESD	64–96	90–110
Chair store		12 – 18

The dining space may also be used for informal school activities, as well as breakfast and after-school clubs.

Some young people need support with eating and may want privacy.

A dining space can also be used for school meetings. Having a place nearby to store furniture when not in use maximises flexibility.

Outdoor spaces

Secondary outdoor activities can encourage children to be adventurous, supporting their skill-based learning and enjoyment of recreational, activities, and supporting their progress to independence. Any conflicting needs should be resolved in the design. A range of spaces should be provided, including:

• outdoor PE facilities

• informal social and recreational areas

• habitat and outdoor classroom areas to support the outdoor curriculum, physical and sensory needs, social and independence skills

Outdoor PE facilities

Many children in special schools can take part in team games and other activities similar to mainstream schools. Some will take part in simplified games for developing throwing, catching and jumping skills.

Outdoor PE facilities typically comprise:

- sports pitches[29] of grass or artificial surfaces
- hard-surfaced games courts such as multi-games, tennis courts, and skill-practice areas

Provision should be geared towards the children at the school - wheelchair users might find using grass pitches more difficult and therefore appropriate 'all weather' surfaces should be considered, which will enable them to take a full part in sporting activities. Although grass pitches are not as useful to some wheelchair users, it is important that the pitches and the access to them are designed and constructed so that wheelchair users can easily and conveniently make full use of them.

The total area of sports pitches and hard-surfaced games courts must add up to at least the minimum required in the Education (School Premises) Regulations 1999. (See Table 24.)

Where special schools are built on restricted sites that cannot comply with the above, access to the curriculum must be ensured by partnership arrangements with other schools and centres.

As a guide, in order to meet the regulations, a secondary special school for a wide range of needs may have:

- one grass pitch of 1200–4018m^2 for various sport or games activities
- one hard court of 700–1400m^2 for netball, basketball or multi-games

A secondary special school for BESD may have:

- one grass pitch of 4698–6016m^2 – medium (87 x 54m) to large (94 x 64m) football pitches – including margins
- one hard court of 1000–1400m^2 for basketball or multi-games

External stores will be needed for play, sports and other curricular equipment and maintenance:

- sports and recreational equipment (about 15m^2)
- smaller external maintenance items (about 10–20m^2)

29. Pitches can be all-weather surfaces or grass, provided they are laid out for playing team games. If grass, it should be capable of sustaining seven hours a week per school during term time. (Rotation allowing grass to recover may be needed.) Refer to the Education (School Premises) Regulations 1999 – http://www.teachernet. gov.uk/ sbregulatoryinformation/

For technical information on all-weather pitches, refer to Sport England's A Guide to the Design, Specification and Construction of Multi Use Games Areas (MUGAs) including Multi-Sport Synthetic Turf Pitches (STPs) – http://www.sportengland. org/facilities_guidance. htm

C

Table 24: Minimum areas for team-game playing fields for all schools	
Total number of pupils aged 8 or over	Area m^2
100 or fewer	5000
101 to 200	10000
201 to 300	15000
Source: The Education (School Premises) Regulations 1999	

Children's needs vary. Some will be very active and others need quieter places. Some children have mobility training in specially laid out areas.

a

b

c

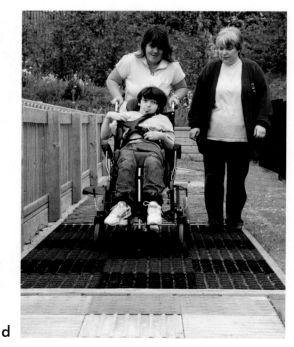

d

Informal social and recreational areas

Access to a separate protected outdoor space for social and recreational use should be provided, using hard and soft surfaced areas. Health and safety are paramount.

Providing a variety of areas for different types of play allows children to make choices and engage in different activities. There may be a need to separate boisterous activities from quieter sheltered spaces for more vulnerable children. There may be:

• space to run, play and kick a ball (a)

• areas with fixed adventure play equipment with safety surfaces (b)

• social spaces with fixed seating to sit and talk, or quiet places to be alone (c)

• areas and routes laid out for mobility training with safe simulations of hazards that children might meet outside school - helping them to develop independence skills (d)

Landscaped paths, fencing and gates, appropriately scaled, could be used to divide areas, to add variety and help with supervision.

The type and amount of sensory stimulus and play equipment will vary according to needs and should be discussed with staff. Wheelchair accessible equipment is available from specialists. All items should be safe and sturdy.

Habitat and outdoor classroom areas

Outdoor learning is mostly experiential and supports work that is different from inside the classroom. There may be:

* a covered outdoor space 2.5m deep, thus extending a classroom on the ground floor

* a suitable external space, 55-65m^2, which may be used as an outdoor classroom

Consulting with staff is essential. For instance, direct external access and views over activity may distract some children and others may want to run off, so a form of access control may be needed. However, access to a safe contained outdoor place may help some children to calm down.

The natural features of any site can provide a rich resource for learning. Grounds can also be enhanced by providing planting, ponds and nature trails – developing them can involve children and staff as part of curriculum activities.

Effective supervision, appropriate sight lines and security are essential to avoid children straying and to provide protection from unauthorised visitors.

Sensory planting, vegetable gardens and greenhouses are important resources and may be developed by older pupils as part of vocational courses.

Useful guidance on outdoor spaces

* Schools for the Future: Designing School Grounds, DfES, 2006 – http://www.teachernet.gov.uk/sbdupublications/

* Designing for Sport on School Sites – http://www.sportengland.org/resource_downloads.htm

* Building Bulletin 98: Briefing Framework for Secondary School Projects – http://www.teachernet.gov.uk/sbareaguidelines/

* Standards for School Premises (guide to the Education (School Premises) Regulations 1999) – http://www.teachernet.gov.uk/sbregulatoryinformation/

* Learning through Landscapes provides advice and guidance - http://www.ltl.org.uk/

Pupils can create their own gardens.

Growing plants can be a sensory experience or part of a vocational course.

Nature and made landscape can provide a rich source of learning material.

C

9 Learning and social spaces – post 16

Post-16 learning

Once statutory education has finished at the age of 16, it is nevertheless still important for young people with SEN and disabilities to develop as far as possible to their full potential, and be recognised as part of the student body.

Some young people work alongside their peers towards nationally recognised, externally accredited qualifications, such as GCSEs, A levels and the new Diplomas. Many in special schools do pre-vocational and vocational qualifications in subjects such as hairdressing, horticulture, catering, care work or trade skills. Some students have their learning and support needs met by an holistic programme of activities, including social skills and independence training.

Young people with SEN and disabilities can progress to further and higher education courses, apprenticeships, employment and/or other suitable education or training.

Typical post-16 spaces in special schools

Accommodation for post–16 provision should be significantly different and separate from that for statutory years. It should allow for activities that reflect the students' approaching adult status and their preparation for progression into the wider community.

Arrangements vary, depending on the local tertiary approach by the LA, school and FE college, but there is often a dedicated post–16 base on the school site, which students use for about half their time for some general activities, including careers guidance and PSHE (personal, social and health education)

Co-located sites

Where post-16 accommodation is co-located with an inclusive sixth form or an FE college, fully accessible facilities and access for learning must be ensured in all cases.

The class base is usually a flexible space, accommodating a range of activities (a). Independence training may be part of the post–16 curriculum (b).

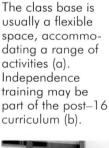

a

b

The post–16 base will typically provide:

• teaching/tutor bases (50–65m²) for small groups of between six and ten students

• small group rooms for support work (15–20m²)

• a student common room (80m²) that provides an informal social and learning space, with kitchen and snack-making facilities, dining tables, chairs and informal low seating. A corner may be laid out as a home setting for learning life skills.

The base will be supported by storage for personal belongings and resources, toilets and changing rooms, as well as staff facilities. (See Support spaces, page 106.)

Since young people post 16 use the special school's practical specialist spaces or the vocational facilities at a local FE college, or work-based training facilities, specialist post–16 provision is rarely made in a special school. However, if such spaces are required, details should be set out clearly in the brief. Typically, spaces range from 50–90m², depending on the type and range of activity. Vocational courses may require there to be additional storage (for example, if course work has to be kept for two years). The design principles for practical specialist subject spaces apply to vocational training spaces.

Facilities for vocational courses may be on site but students often attend a local FE college. The Learning and Skills Council has useful design guidance on spaces for vocational courses at http://designguid-ance.lsc.gov.uk/

Table 25: Typical post–16 spaces	
Spaces	Area m²
Teaching/tutor base	50–65
Small group room	15–20
Student common room	40–80
Practical/vocational space	50–90

10 Support spaces – all schools

This section sets out the accommodation that may be needed in primary and secondary mainstream and special schools to support children and young people with SEN and disabilities and the school workforce:

- Medical, therapy and other support
- Staff accommodation
- Storage
- Toilets and changing facilities
- Kitchens

Table 26 gives recommended areas for a typical range of support spaces in a mainstream school, in addition to small group rooms. Schools will not necessarily have all these facilities. Requirements at a particular school will depend on children's needs.

Table 26: Typical support spaces – mainstream		
	Primary m^2	Secondary m^2
SENCo office/interview	8–12	8–15
Multi-agency office	12–15	12–15
First aid/sick bay	9–16	9–16
Medical MI/therapy	15–20	15–20
Multi-use therapy/support	20–30	20–30
Meeting/teaching room	16–20	16–25
Accessible toilet/change	12–16	18–30
(number depends on school size)		

Typical areas are given as guidance.
The upper range allows more circulation space for wheelchair users.

30. Including Me: Managing Complex Health Needs in Schools and Early Years Settings, Council for Disabled Children and Department for Education and Skills – http://www.ncb.org.uk/resources/

10a Medical, therapy and other support

The range of professionals (full-time or sessional) working with children with special needs and disabilities, wherever they go to school, will vary but may include:

- school nurse
- visiting doctor
- physiotherapists
- occupational therapists
- speech and language therapists
- specialists for hearing and visual impairment and mobility officers
- psychiatric support
- social workers
- educational psychologists
- counsellors

Range of spaces

Some medical and therapeutic tasks can and should be carried out within a teaching space. Others have to happen away from the class group, sometimes in a specialist space. For example, medical treatment requires hygienic facilities and privacy. The timetabling and use of such specialist support spaces depends on the type and level of therapeutic input, as well as the need for privacy and quiet.

There are three main types of provision:

- Medical facilities (e.g. medical inspection room required by School Premises Regulations, first aid room)

- Therapy rooms to support healthcare and children's access to education (e.g. physiotherapy, hydrotherapy[30])

- Admin spaces for multi-agency professionals (e.g. offices, case conference and meeting rooms) See Staff accommodation page 117.

All schools have medical inspection and first aid facilities[31]. The range of other spaces (some of which might be multi-functional), which will be set down in the brief, will depend on the children catered for at a particular school.

Mainstream schools may have a multi-purpose therapy/support space of around 20–30m². In some cases a mainstream school may also have one or more of the spaces listed in Table 27, possibly associated with resourced provision or a designated unit.

Special schools have a greater number and wider range of specialist support spaces. Recommended areas for typical spaces are given in Table 27. These spaces are described in more detail below. Ideally, medical and therapy rooms should be entered off a lobby or corridor, avoiding rooms off other rooms (which causes disruption).

Table 27: Typical medical and therapy spaces – special schools	
Space	Area m²
Medical room	15–25
School nurse	15–20
Store – sundries	2 – 4
Store – oxygen cylinders	2 – 4
Physiotherapy/shared use for therapy	25–30
Store	4–10
Speech and language therapy	12–15
Audiology	20–24
Observation room	10–12
Audiology technician	20–30
VI resource	40–60
VI technician	16–20
VI mobility training room	20–50
Sensory room	12–24
Sensory studio	50–60
Hydrotherapy	85
Warm water pool	144
Soft play	24–30
Social/recreational	50–60
Social skills	20–25

31. Employers must provide adequate and appropriate equipment, facilities and qualified first aid personnel under the Health and Safety (First Aid Regulations 1981), as well as suitable and sufficient accommodation for first aid according to the first aid needs identified. Staff, pupils and visitors are not included in risk assessments for first aid needs. Refer to DCSF guidance on first aid for schools – http://www.teachernet. gov.uk/wholeschool/ healthandsafety/firstaid/

C

Medical rooms

All schools must have a designated space for visiting medical staff and the treatment and care of children. There also needs to be somewhere for first aid emergencies and where a sick person can be closely supervised by a member of staff [32].

In mainstream schools, a space of 12–18m^2 may be suitable as a medical room that might also be used for therapy, as long as first aid emergencies can be dealt with in, say, a sick bay elsewhere. If a greater level of support is required (likely in many special schools), a medical room of 15–25m^2 is recommended.

The medical room(s) should be close to other therapy facilities. Some schools have a suite of rooms with toilet and changing facilities close by. There must be easy access for emergency services and enough circulation space for larger wheelchairs and trolleys.

There need to be:

• window and door security (to protect medicines and confidential records)

• non-abrasive wall surfaces and slip resistant floor surfaces that are easy to clean and maintain for good standards of hygiene

• appropriate furniture and equipment, such as a desk and chairs, an adjustable couch, a treatment trolley, a filing cabinet and lockable cupboard and/or fridge for drugs[33], clinical

wash-hand basin, some soft furnishings and shelves

• visual privacy for general medical examination, with portable screens, blinds or curtains

• good sound insulation for privacy (with specialist acoustic treatment for hearing testing, if necessary)

• ceiling-mounted or portable mobile hoists with the area needed for their use

• enough length for vision testing

• a suitable place for resting or recovery after a seizure (if required) (Space requirements should be assessed if there is a need for resuscitation and equipment.)

• secure storage for confidential records, with ICT for secure back-up

• safe disposal of clinical waste, contaminated material and 'sharps'(injection-syringe needles), such as by the use of the yellow bag system and sharps containers (as required by the PCT)

• good quality natural and artificial lighting for general and detailed work, with dimmable local controls and a task light or medical lamp for examinations

• rapid-extract ventilation to eliminate unwanted smells

• appropriate levels of heating and cooling, with easily adjustable local controls

Some special schools, for example when children have profound and multiple learning difficulties, may have a second room of 15–20m^2 as a nurse's base and for preparing gastro-tube feed. (The facilities required for this should be discussed with staff and set out in the brief but are likely to include a wash-hand basin, refrigeration and/or thermostatic heating facilities.)

32. Under the Education (Schools Premises) Regulations 1999 (SPRs), all schools must have accommodation for the medical or dental examination and treatment of pupils and the care of sick or injured pupils.

33. Drugs (especially controlled drugs) must be stored to comply with COSHH, with a lockable cupboard, fridge and alarmed access. They may be in a separate room not accessible to children. Refer to: Managing Medicines in Schools and Early Years Settings – http://publications. teachernet.gov.uk/

Physiotherapy

In a school setting, a physiotherapist carries out assessments and devises treatment plans, working with teaching and support assistants to instruct them on how to deliver programmes to meet the needs of children individually or in small groups.

Some physiotherapy can be carried out in the corner of a teaching space or SEN resource base, set out with matting and mirrors (which should be protected). Alternatively, it may take place in one of the following:

• a multi-purpose support space (25–30m²) (if suitably fitted out, e.g. with a couch, a clinical wash hand basin, and a curtained or screened changing space)

• a large medical room (18–25m²) with an adjustable height couch and equipped with a ceiling-mounted hoist (If portable hoists are used, 25–30m² may be needed.)

• a fully equipped physiotherapy room (25–30m² is recommended) – where there is a higher level of need it may also be used by other therapists, as appropriate, on a timetabled basis

Storage space (4–10 m²) will be needed to support any of these spaces, for inflatables, physical aids and equipment. It should be directly accessible from the space, with outward-opening doors.

A physiotherapy room should be robust and functional, daylit, with a pleasant outlook. The walls and ceiling construction will need to be able to support the fixing and use of hoists and the force involved in children pulling themselves up on equipment. Wall and floor finishes need to be easily maintained and have visual contrast.

The room should have enough clear space for the therapist to work and to transfer a child from a wheelchair using a hoist, where appropriate. (See page 164.) There will also need to be space for the use and storage of equipment such as wheelchairs and standing frames, and for:

• a clinical wash-hand basin

• display, full-height mirrors and parallel bars

• an adjustable height electrically operated therapy couch (about 900 x 1800mm minimum)

• a desk, PC and a lockable filing cabinet (although sometimes this could be part of a centralised visiting professionals' office)

There should be an accessible toilet/changing room nearby.

Occupational therapy

Occupational therapists (OTs) in school settings advise on learning aids, ICT requirements, furniture, equipment and environmental adaptations for the school and home, usually in a teaching space, group room, or therapy base. For older children developing independent living skills, the post–16 tutorial or social base may be used. Storage facilities for rehabilitation equipment may be needed. OTs will also use the visiting professionals' office.

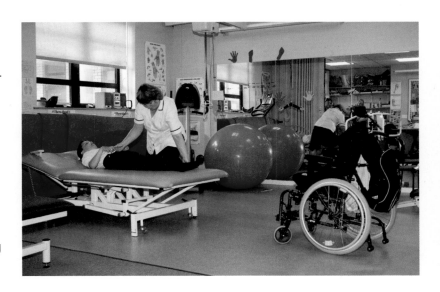

Speech and language therapy

The speech and language therapist (SLT) works with children in the classroom or a separate quiet room. Sometimes a dedicated speech and language therapy base is provided[34].

A room of 12–15m² will support individual or small group work. For larger groups of between six and eight, a space of 39–65m² may be needed.

A room for SLT will typically need:

- a desk and chairs
- personal computer
- lockable filing cabinet
- full-height storage cupboard (for records and resources)
- free wall space for visual display
- a mirror for speech articulation work
- a wash-hand basin
- good quality lighting
- blinds to windows
- good quality acoustics and sound insulation
- an induction loop or hearing aid facilities

Allowances may also need to be made for specialist SLT aids, audio visual equipment and children's communication aids. A large number of electrical and/or electronic power points and battery-charging outlets will be needed.

Hearing impairment support

Sometimes there are specialist facilities in special schools for children with hearing impairment. In mainstream schools, the sensory impairment support service may use a small group room, as long as it is quiet and provides suitable acoustic conditions[35].

An audiology suite may also have dual use for speech and language therapy.

An audiology room (20–24m²) will be used for testing and assessing children with hearing impairment. It may be combined with an observation room (10–12m²), with a one-way window in between for training purposes.

Audiology rooms need to have a high degree of sound insulation from adjacent spaces. The reverberation time and level of sound absorption within the space will depend on the equipment used. There may need to be triple-glazed windows, acoustic-lined walls and ceiling and an acoustic floating floor. Appropriate heating and ventilation will also be needed.

Sound-proofed accommodation should be provided to ISO 8253-1 (1987) and ISO 8253-2 (1992) standards for acoustic test methods suitable for children[36].

An audiology technician's room (20–30 m²) may be needed nearby for storage, testing and repairing small equipment.

34. Refer to: The Royal College of Speech and Language Therapists guidance on accommodation and equipment for speech and language therapy in Communicating Quality – http://www.rcslt.org/resources/

35 Refer to: the National Deaf Children's Society for specialist advice – http://www.ndcs.org.uk/

36. Building Bulletin 93 Acoustic Design for Schools – http://www.teachernet.gov.uk//sbdupublications/

Visual impairment support

Children with visual impairment have mobility training and also need to use specialist resources, such as Braille, large print books and ICT.

A VI resource space of 40–60m² typically provides adequate space for the preparation of VI resources, for using a number of different types of machines and ICT equipment, as well as for a large layout space. There should be good quality lighting and blinds, and adequate electrical power points and data cabling. Adjustable height shelving will be needed for storing large print documents, which take up considerable space (c).

a

A mobility training room (20–50m²) needs a range of kitchen units with specially adapted fittings, as well as a table and chairs (b). A large open space may be needed with tactile surfaces on the wall and floor for mobility training. Mobility training can also take place around the school and/or in an external area designed for the purpose (for example with different surfaces and obstacles for young people to learn to negotiate).

b

A technician's room (16–20m²) may be needed, with space for servicing and using equipment (a).

c

C

Sensory spaces

Multi-sensory spaces contain light, sound and other equipment for multi-sensory work.

Sensory rooms, used for one-to-one and small group work, are highly resourced spaces, often entirely white or black, which use a range of equipment to create different light, sound and other stimuli for multi-sensory work. Mirrors and mirror balls, bubble tubes, fibre optics and interactive switch equipment are often used (but too many stimuli may confuse or limit effective use).

'Dark rooms' tend to have black walls and ceilings and/or perimeter black curtaining to support light-stimulation work for a child with very poor vision. Visually tracking moving lights can help children develop coordination skills.

Provision varies but typically a school may have one large white room of 24–32m² or two small rooms of 12–16m² to provide separate 'light' or 'dark' rooms. Some schools may choose to create a temporary sensory environment in the corner of a learning space. Typically for sensory rooms there should be:

- a clear area just inside the door, with enough space for the removal of shoes or outer clothing

- sufficient clear space to transfer from wheelchairs (by hoist) to the main cushioned platform area

- an appropriate ceiling height and construction for overhead hoists (2.6–2.8m high is suitable, see page 164.)

- plastic covered cushioned linings to walls, to half or full height (fire-rated foam products should be checked for health, safety and fire prevention with the supplier)

- wall construction that can support wall-linings, shelving and specialist equipment

- a firm slip-resistant floor, with soft carpet or cushioned sheet flooring

- furnishings and equipment that are safe, durable, easily maintained, with appropriate use of colour

- no sharp edges or projections that could cause harm

- blind and black-out facilities

- dimmer switches to adjust light levels

- plentiful power and data supplies for electrical equipment, positioned for adult use (usually at high level), with a switch control panel and avoiding trailing leads

- materials that allow for frequent cleaning

Sensory studios are larger multi-sensory spaces (50–60m^2) for individual and whole class groups. They may be fitted as a large white room, or as a studio with some bench seating, where curriculum delivery and therapy can be carried out. In some schools such a space may also be used for drama activities. Typical equipment includes an interactive whiteboard, large wall projection, DVD/video/television, sound and light projectors and smoke effects. There should be local temperature controls.

Consultation with staff and specialist firms is essential to ensure suitable and safe installations. The outcomes of health and safety assessments should also be incorporated in the design.

C

Sensory studios may be flexible multi-functional spaces or fitted out with specialist equipment as here.

Hydrotherapy

Hydrotherapy is included in some special schools, principally for treatment and exercise for students with physical and/or sensory disabilities. Warm water provides an effective medium for muscle relaxation and is a pleasurable, therapeutic experience that may encourage the development of communication and interaction skills.

Work is undertaken in a small group or on a one-to-one basis with a physiotherapist or another adult, with careful supervision provided by an out-of-water adult.

Types of pool

A typical hydrotherapy pool needs an overall space of 85m², with:

• a pool of 24m²

• a surround of 2–2.5m wide (ensuring safe movement)

37. Management of Spa Pools – Controlling the Risks of Infection, Health Protection Agency and the Health and Safety Executive – http://www.hpa.org.uk/publications

Andy Major Photography

The following spaces are also needed:

• wet changing areas for pupils – 30m² each for boys and girls separately

• staff changing of 4m² to 6m² each for males and females separately

• pool plant and chemical storage of about 20m² and 6m² respectively

A warm water pool, which is larger than a hydrotherapy pool and different water temperature, may be installed in some special schools. It provides for hydrotherapy and also for school group recreational activities. A space of up to 144m² may be required, with a pool size of 72m².

Sometimes smaller learner/training pools are also installed. These are shallow warm water pools about 12–18m long and 4–6m wide, with two or three 2m wide lanes and with a typical depth of 0.9m. Larger changing rooms and staff facilities may be needed, depending on the type and extent of use.

Spa pools or splash pools are not usually installed, since there are concerns about pollution and maintenance[37].

In some cases, a larger (possibly joint funded) combined pool facility will support the school's PE programme, as well as having restricted use by designated groups, such as health charity and community users. The implications of community use should be considered from the start. It is not appropriate to use a pool designated for hydrotherapy for general swimming because of the high risk of pollution, the cost of maintenance and the reduced availability to disabled children.

See Warm water/hydrotherapy pools, page 156, for more detail.

Educational psychology, psychotherapy and counselling

Visiting educational psychologists, psychotherapists and counsellors normally use a small group room, or similar. Such small rooms need a balance between privacy and quiet for confidentiality, and visibility for overseeing students, safety and security. For example, a fixed glazed panel in the door and in the wall, with internal blinds, may be provided.

Other interventions and therapies

Schools may have other visiting specialist professionals, such as complementary therapists.

Generally, all other visiting professionals use existing accommodation such as the medical or therapy, small-group/ quiet room, or interview room and the visiting professionals' office.

Suitable safe storage of materials is needed to avoid fire hazards. Good ventilation and/or rapid extraction may also be needed.

Appropriate safe and hygienic soft furnishings can help to create an appropriate ambience.
(See FF&E, page 160.)

Soft play rooms

Soft play rooms allow children (for example, with SLD/PMLD/ASD) to move without inhibition and fear of injury. The walls and floor of the play area are usually lined with soft-padded mats covered in non-abrasive, non-absorbent, cleanable, resilient materials, such as plastic-coated foam. There are usually shapes or toys of the same material. A room of at least 24m^2 will allow for lively, robust play. The space should be naturally lit and ventilated (from high-level windows opening outwards) wherever possible, and internal spaces should be avoided.

Advice should be obtained from specialist suppliers on the detailed design but the following are important:

• No sharp corners or breakable fittings

• Fire-rated foam products used checked with suppliers

• Materials that allow for strict cleaning procedures

• A clear area inside the door, with a resilient, easily cleaned floor covering and adequate space for the removal of shoes and to hang outer clothing

• Clear circulation space for wheelchairs and for safe transfer onto the soft play area, using a hoist

• A ceiling height that allows for a ceiling-mounted hoist travelling in both directions for access to all parts of the space, but avoiding light fittings or mobiles

• Suitable safe specialist lighting and music systems

Social skills training

Some schools (particularly those with children who have BESD) have one or more rooms for social skills training. Typically there is one room of around 20-25m² per key stage, equipped with typical domestic furniture.

Social/recreational activity space

A social/recreational activity space can be used on a structured basis or as part of a reward system for good behaviour in a special school or resourced provision for children with BESD.

A space of 50–60m² can be arranged for playing table tennis, snooker, table football and board games, with informal seating. Attractive robust finishes, fittings and furnishings should be easily cleanable and offer no opportunities for self-harm.

Calming rooms

These small rooms are used to help children calm down. Good sight lines, health, safety and welfare must be ensured. A pleasant calm space is needed. Materials, fittings and finishes should safeguard against self-harm.

Parents' rooms

A parents' room is often provided near the reception area. A typical space is around 15m², with a small worktop, sink and fridge, informal seating, a low table, book/magazine shelves and display boards.

10b Staff accommodation[38]

The quality of staff accommodation can affect staff performance as well as their recruitment and retention. A well designed environment can help to minimise stress and contribute to the effective and efficient running of the school.

The number and range of staff (including visiting and peripatetic staff, extended school and community staff), school organisation and ethos all affect accommodation needs.
Designers need to bear in mind:

- the greater numbers of all staff usually required to support children and young people with SEN or disabilities

- provision for outreach facilities, since both mainstream and special schools have an important role to play in the local school and wider communities

- special schools as an important resource for the wider educational community - increasing numbers will come either to learn or to use its resources, so areas will need to accommodate other teachers, therapists and visitors

- the particular need for staff teaching and supporting children with SEN and disabilities to liaise with each other, sometimes confidentially – they need places to meet, paging or panic alarm systems, CCTV, ICT and video conferencing

- balancing the need for visual and acoustic confidentiality in all spaces with the need for openness, transparency and accountability (i.e. the need to see and be seen to act and behave appropriately)

Co-location

The extent to which staff will share facilities will need to be established at the briefing stage.

Typical staff spaces

Table 28 lists a typical range of staff spaces in a special school. The spaces are described in more detail below.

Storage associated with these spaces needs to be assessed, whether in the space itself or in an adjacent store room. (See page 121.)

Table 28: Staff accommodation – special schools[39]	
Space	Area m^2
Reception/admin office	20
Head teacher's office	15–18
Deputy head teacher's office	10–15
Visiting professionals' office	15
Meeting/training room (outreach)	20–25
Premises manager's office	10
Staff room (depending on staff numbers)	40–60
Staff preparation/(depending on staff numbers)	20–30
Technicians' space	varies
Cleaners' room (number varies)	2
Staff changing room and lockers (separate male and female) depending on staff numbers	20–40
Staff changing room near pool (separate male and female)	8
Staff changing room near hall (separate male and female)	8
Disabled toilets (number varies)	4
Staff toilets (separate male and female) depending on staff numbers	16–24

38. Schools have to comply with the Health and Safety at Work Act 1974 and associated legislation.

Also refer to the HSC Workplace (Health, Safety and Welfare) Regulations 1992 approved code of practice, and, in particular, Regulation 10.

Refer to the HSE's Health and safety regulation...... a short guide – http://www.hse.gov.uk/pubns/hsc13.pdf

39. For guidance on staff accommodation in mainstream schools, refer to:
Building Bulletin 98, Briefing Framework for Secondary School Projects and
Building Bulletin 99, Briefing Framework for Primary School Projects – http://www.teachernet.gov.uk/sbareaguidelines/

C

A meeting area in or adjacent to the head teacher's office is a valuable resource.

Deputy heads usually have their own office for quiet working, one-to-one meetings etc.

An attractive outside space provides an alternative social/meeting place.

Reception/admin office

A combined space for reception and admin is usual, with sufficient space for between three and five members of staff to work comfortably, including clearances for circulation. It needs storage space, including for secure storage of records and the safe storage of flammable or toxic materials kept in this area, along with the main communications network, security, CCTV and alarm systems.

Senior staff offices

The head teacher's office is usually located near the school entrance and the reception/administration office. An office of 15–18m^2 will typically be sufficient to allow for general use and meetings.

Senior staff offices are usually near reception and the head teacher, or in another strategic location.

If the school has one or more deputy head teacher, they will need an office (12–15m^2) for admin and for small meetings. Heads and deputies will be holding confidential meetings, so privacy and quiet are important. There need to be adjustable blinds on any glazed screens and windows, and good acoustic insulation.

Site management staff

The premises manager or caretaker will need an office and workshop facilities for undertaking small repairs. A centrally, electronically controlled environmental services system may be used, such as a Building Management System (BMS).

Meeting and training rooms

During the school day, teachers and support assistants must have unlimited access to their own meeting room. There will probably need to be one or more additional spaces for meetings or training sessions for use by school staff, visiting staff or parents and carers. An area of 25m² will meet most of these needs.

These spaces will be most flexible if they are located together and can be rearranged to suit varied activities. Typical furniture and equipment includes loose tables and chairs, audio-visual and ICT facilities, and blackout.

Visiting professionals' office

Visiting professional staff need a base from which to carry out admin work. The office will need to be at least 15m², with storage for each professional.

Staff room

The staff room size is determined by the total number of staff who use it at the same time, the frequency of use and the number of meetings held there. Large meetings tend to take place in a separate space.

There need to be workstations, notice boards, book/magazine shelves, audio-visual facilities with blinds and blackout and a small area for refreshments.

Local staff spaces may be required for nurseries or designated units.

Staff preparation and resource space

A separate resource and preparation area for teaching and support staff to plan and prepare programmes of work is usually located with other staff rooms, its size governed by the number of staff and the need for

visiting teachers to store equipment and resources associated with their professional roles.

Reprographics space

It is good practice for reprographics equipment for teaching support and admin staff to be located near to staff office or work areas. There needs to be enough space for photocopiers, audio-visual equipment and any specialist equipment.

Many meetings take place in special schools, often involving staff from other schools and agencies.

Visiting staff need access to a desk, computer and secure storage.

The staff room should be a comfortable and attractive space for staff to rest and meet informally.

Technicians' specialist spaces

Technical support is required for a range of subjects such as science or design and technology, so specialist prep or resources rooms need to be provided. See individual learning spaces earlier in the book.

Specialist SEN technicians may be employed to manage equipment and services, such as for ICT, mobility and auditory and visual impairment aids provided in SEN technical or resources space. There should be sufficient space to work on large items, with enough room for a workbench and storage. (See also Hearing impairment support, page 110, and Visual impairment support, page 111.)

Some children use a range of equipment that needs to be stored when not in use. This may be in a technician's room or resource base. (See HI and VI support, pages 110 and 111.)

40. Refer to Accessible Sports Facilities – http://www.sportengland. org/facilities_guidance. htm

Cleaners

In addition to cleaners' stores, cleaning staff should have access to lockers, accessible changing and toilet facilities, and suitable spaces (such as a staff room) for breaks and refreshments, as appropriate.

Toilets and changing rooms

There should be sufficient and suitable staff toilet and changing room spaces, including wheelchair-accessible facilities, depending on the number of staff and the male/female ratio, which should be stated in the brief. Typical facilities include:

- separate male and female staff toilets and changing rooms, with secure locker storage for personal belongings

- unisex accessible toilets (providing these throughout the school helps to minimise staff absence from the classroom)

- changing rooms for PE, with a bench and coat hooks, toilet and shower, located adjacent to the PE/hall space and ideally drama spaces to avoid duplication

- unisex accessible staff changing rooms with accessible toilet and shower areas

- unisex accessible staff wet changing facilities for hydrotherapy, with accessible toilet and shower

- sufficient and suitable toilet and changing spaces, including accessible facilities, for inter-school events, visitors and users of extended school and community services. Depending on the school, its use, zoning and management, unisex facilities can be used by visitors[40].

All staff members should have their own secure locker in a staff changing area and a coat hook in the class store.

10c Storage

Having enough well placed storage space is vital to support learning, teaching and school management. Children with SEN and disabilities can benefit particularly. For example:

- Appropriate storage can help to reduce distractions in the class base and minimise movement of young people or furniture.

- Some children with autistic spectrum disorder require individual storage as part of a teaching strategy - mobile base units or baskets on shelves may be needed for these children.

- Children with multiple disabilities may need space for temporary storage for their personal, communication and medical aids and their personal belongings and learning resources wherever they go.

It is important to assess storage requirements at the earliest stage and ensure the design solution meets these needs, considering:

- what is being stored

- storage method (e.g. walk-in store or cupboards)

- location of storage (e.g. adjacent to a particular space)

- access needs (e.g. whether resources are used daily or only periodically)

Sufficient storage space needs to be allowed for – and retained – in the gross area calculations (storage area requirements are often underestimated)

Typical storage needs

Pupils' belongings

Storage for pupils' belongings is required by the Education (School Premises) Regulations 1999. The type of provision, its accessibility and security should be considered in relation to the phase of education and individual need.

Lockers or lockable cupboards may be provided where security is essential. If required, spare clothes are normally kept within the toilet/changing areas.

Pupils can access their lockers more easily if they are in common areas. Lockers must not impede circulation routes.

Some schools prefer to have resources stored in the classroom where access can be supervised, rather than in a nearby store. Allowance must be made for accessing the storage when calculating room areas.

Mobility aids
Mobility aids take up a considerable amount of room, with up to three bulky items of equipment per person. As a general rule, it is best to avoid narrow deep storage spaces, which are more difficult to access. Shallow bays along circulation routes are useful for storing mobility equipment and belongings in lockers. Some schools prefer enclosed spaces and a central equipment store may be required.

Medical and communication aids and equipment
Some children (for example those with visual or hearing impairment) use specialist equipment that will need to be stored in a technical or resource base. (See Hearing impairment support, page 110, and Visual impairment support, page 111.)

Learning and teaching resources and equipment
Plentiful storage is needed for learning and teaching resources and equipment next to the relevant activity area. Some equipment (such as for PE, music and drama) is particularly large. If wheelchair sports are to be played, it is important that convenient and secure storage is allowed for the sports chairs.

Dangerous chemicals
Dangerous chemicals need to be stored safely, in compliance with COSHH regulations. Stores that may contain these harmful materials should be identified and health and safety risk assessments made. Special ventilation and fire protection and detection measures may also be required[41].

Confidential papers, documents and records
Secure storage is needed for confidential papers, medical records and historical records or documents that may need to be retained in a safe place for a number of years.

Fire-resistant cabinets, cupboards or store rooms with special locking devices may be required.

Medical goods, medicines and dangerous drugs or chemicals
Medicines and drugs should be stored securely according to health and safety requirements. For example, a fridge with a lock and a double-locked drug cupboard may be required in the medical room.

Oxygen in cylinders needs to be stored in a ventilated, secure internal or external store, with access and egress for delivery and collection[42].

Furniture
Storage may be needed for loose furniture. A chair store is usually provided directly off the dining or hall space.

Extended school and community use
There may need to be additional and separate storage of resources and equipment associated with community or extended school use.

Bulk storage
Bulk storage is needed for stationery and admin supplies, general teaching supplies and dry goods.

Kitchen stores
See page 135.

External stores
External storage is needed for:

- bikes, play and sports equipment

- maintenance and landscaping equipment

- technicians' work or a caretaker's base for repairs/maintenance for the school buildings

- large refuse bins or paladins, accessible for collection but screened from general view

- material for recycling, in suitable containers to avoid fire

42. For more information on the use and storage of oxygen cylinders, refer to the HSE's Take Care with Oxygen – http://www.hse.gov.uk/pubns/hse8.pdf

41. Refer to COSHH regulations, http://www.hse.gov.uk/coshh/

Table 29: Typical storage requirements for a broad-range special school with 100 pupils

Space	Number and type	Area m² Primary	Area m² Secondary
Coats and bags	1 per class base	2	2
Mobility equipment bays	1 per class base	10 per bay	10 per bay
General teaching/class base	1 per class base	4	4
Food technology	1 general (+1 food)	3	4 + 4
Design and technology	1 resource (+1 work in progress)	4	8 + 7
ICT (excluding server)	1 general	4	4
Library	1 general store	4	4
SEN resource base store	1	4	4
Art	1 resource (+1 work in progress)	included in D&T	7 + 6
Science	1 prep/store	included in D&T	15
Music and drama	1	8	10
Physical education	1	10	18
Dining	1 furniture	10	15
Community	1	8	8
Common room	1 store	n/a	4
Kitchen	1 food (+ 1 refuse)	6 + 6	6 + 6
Therapy	1	4	4
Hydrotherapy	1 chemical storage	6	6
Medical/communications aids/equipment	1	5	5
Oxygen cylinders	2	2	2
Visiting professionals' office	1	2	2
Administration	stationery + secure records	4	4
Central teaching resource	1	20	20
Meeting/training room	1 resource	2	2
Cleaner	2	2	2
Premises	1	9	9
General stores	1 bulk items	10	10
External stores	1 PE/play (+ 1 maintenance)	10 + 20	15 + 20

C

Table 30: Typical storage requirements for a BESD special school with 50 pupils

Space	Number and type	Area m² Primary	Area m² Secondary
Coats and bags (secondary may be in lockers)	1 per class base	2	2
General teaching/class base	1 per class base	4	4
Food technology	1 general (+1 food)	3	4 + 4
Design and technology	1 resource (+1 work in progress)	4	8 + 7
ICT (excluding server)	1 general	4	4
Library	1 general store	4	4
Art	1 resource (+1 work in progress)	included in D&T	7 + 6
Science	1 prep	included in D&T	15
Music and drama	1	8	10
Physical education	1	12	30
Dining	1 furniture	8	8
Community	1	8	8
Common room	1 store	n/a	4
Social skills base	2	1	1
Kitchen	1 food (+1 refuse)	6 + 6	6 + 6
Visiting professional's office	1	2	2
Administration	stationery + secure records	4 + 4	4 + 4
Central teaching resource	1	14	14
Meeting/training room	1 resource	2	2
Cleaner	2	2	2
Premises	1	9	9
General stores	1 bulk items	10	10
External stores	1 PE/play (+1 maintenance)	10 + 20	15 + 20

10d Toilets and changing facilities

Toilets and hygiene rooms

Provision depend on children's needs and the school's approach to managing toileting arrangements. Schools are likely to have some combination of:

- changing facilities for the very young
- standard toilet cubicles
- larger toilet cubicles for children who need more space to use training aids, or to move around using mobility aids
- wheelchair-accessible toilets
- specially equipped hygiene rooms for changing and showering some children with severe physical or profound and multiple disabilities (PD/PMLD)

Some children need access to a medical room for privacy, assistance or training.

The provision must meet the minimum standards of the Education (School Premises) Regulations 1999 and may have to exceed this in order to meet local needs and achieve good practice standards. (See references above.) There should be enough flexibility to allow for variations in occupancy.

There need to be:

- separate facilities from those for staff and/or visitors (although shared unisex accessible facilities are permitted in some cases)
- separate facilities for younger and older children in all-age schools
- separate toilet provision for boys and girls aged eight and above (and ideally for hygiene rooms too)

The decision whether to have urinals (individual or communal) should be made with the client and/or staff. Where urinals are provided, these should be installed at an age-appropriate height and at least some (depending on children's needs) should have grab rails to ensure they are accessible to those who are non-ambulant.

If there is a risk of toilets being blocked with paper towels, warm-air hand driers can be used but cross-infection risks and energy use should be assessed.

Regulations and guidance

The Education (School Premises) Regulations 1999 require that facilities must be adequate, having regard to the age, sex and numbers of the pupils and any special requirements they may have.

SPRs require at least one shower, bath or deep sink for every 40 pupils under 5. Deep sinks have health and safety risks for manual handling and infection control – http://www.teachernet.gov.uk/sbregulatoryinformation/

Standards for School Premises (DfEE 0029/2000) clarifies the SPRs requirements – http://www.teachernet.gov.uk/sbregulatoryinformation/

Approved Document M of the Building Regulations (2004), Access to and use of buildings – http://www.planningportal.gov.uk/buildingregulations

BS 8300: Design of buildings and their approaches to meet the needs of disabled people 2005 (adults) – http://www.bsi-global.com/shop

BS 6465: Sanitary installations – http://www.bsi-global.com/shop

Changing Places http://www.changing-places.org/

Standard specifications, layouts and dimensions (SSLD) 3: toilets in schools – http://www.teachernet.gov.uk/management/resourcesfinanceandbuilding/schoolbuildings/innovativedesign/standardspecifications/

HSE's Health and Safety Matters for SEN: Moving and Handling 2005 – http://www.hse.gov.uk/pubns/edis4.pdf

School Inclusion Design Brief Appendix H of Hampshire County Council's Accessibility Strategy – http://www.hants.gov.uk/education/department/strategy/accessibility/

C

Location

Accessible toilet and changing facilities should be conveniently located around the school to avoid loss of curriculum time and supervision problems.

In early years, toilets and changing areas are generally located directly off the play space.

For primary and secondary settings, toilet and changing accommodation is usually reached from a circulation space. However, some younger primary age children can find enclosed WC cubicles off the corridor intimidating. Supervision must be balanced with the fact that travelling to the toilet can develop independence skills for children with SEN and disabilities. A travel distance of not more than 20–25 metres is recommended[43].

Routes should be easy to navigate, with suitable wayfinding. There should be clear sightlines to the toilet space to prevent children from wandering. For older children, hidden spaces should be avoided where inappropriate behaviour could occur.

For some children with severe disabilities, continence is a big problem and having access to a WC in the immediate vicinity of the classroom is key. As many disabled children may need the toilet immediately on arrival at school, the travel distances from the drop-off point to the nearest accessible WC should be minimised.

A wheelchair accessible toilet can be provided either within each of the boys' and girls' toilet spaces or separately, possibly as a unisex provision. An accessible WC may be provided within the hygiene room. (This also provides choice for those children who feel confined in a cubicle with high partitions, or a separate toilet room.) Unisex accessible toilet provision should be provided for any community use/parental visits where someone from the opposite sex may need to provide assistance.

Laundry

In most special schools, a self-contained laundry facility is required. This could be a room of about 6–8m^2, depending on its use. Provision can be made centrally, or with separate spaces sited adjacent to, but separate from, changing rooms.

An arrangement where machines fit under a worktop with spare clothes storage in boxes on shelves above avoids mixing of clothes. Usually large commercial washing machines and drying machines are installed because of the intensive and frequent use.

Disposal of waste products

The arrangements for the removal of waste (soiled nappies/liners or sanitary products, soiled dressings) and for the transfer of soiled clothes to the laundry should be described in the brief to ensure hygienic arrangements. Designers need to consider the accommodation implications (for example, space for storing waste prior to collection). Some schools still prefer macerators in hygiene areas. This is a local decision but they would need to

43. In the Building Regulations Approved Document M, the maximum travel distance for disabled adults is 40m. Refer to: http://www.planningportal.gov.uk/buildingregulations

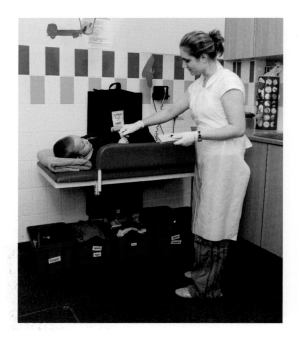

An adjustable changing bed in an early years setting

be used and maintained properly and the impact on drainage needs should be considered.

Toilets and hygiene rooms – key design points

Toilets and changing rooms should be designed with the following in mind. Typical examples are shown on pages 128–131 but designs should be discussed and agreed with staff.

• There should be enough room for non-ambulant children to move around and for staff (at least two adults for a secondary age child using a wheelchair), to help them if necessary, taking account of manual handling and transfer arrangements, including the use of portable or mobile hoists. Space is also needed to store the hoist and wheelchair when not in use. (See Technical section – Hoists, page 164.)

• Fixtures and fittings should be robust and at an appropriate height (some may need to be height adjustable) and within easy reach of users. For wheelchair users, wash-hand basins may be adjustable height or fixed height with a knee recess.

• The layout, fixtures and fittings should reflect the age of the children and help them develop personal care skills. For example, children in early years settings have lower-height cubicles and smaller toilet fittings.

• Screening needs to allow for supervision while maintaining children's privacy.

• Where a school has pupils with motor disabilities, particular attention needs to be paid to fittings such as taps. Long lever handles or infra-red fittings may overcome these difficulties. Soap dispensers and towel dispensers should be specified and positioned to encourage their use, considering both dexterity and reach.

Adjustable height wash hand basins and lever taps may be needed.

C

Accessible toilets – examples of provision

The diagrams below and opposite can be used as a guide. Reference should also be made to the regulations and guidance documents listed on page 125.

Plans showing three types of accessible toilet meeting the standards of BS 8300. Outward opening doors shown in each case are preferable for safety.

• For ambulant disabled children (a)
• A corner layout (which independent users, prefer for greater support) for independent wheelchair users, allowing some assistance if required (b). It is advisable to provide some for left handed and some for right handed transfer arrangements.
• A peninsular layout allowing staff to assist both sides. The wider unit may be preferred in a secondary school.

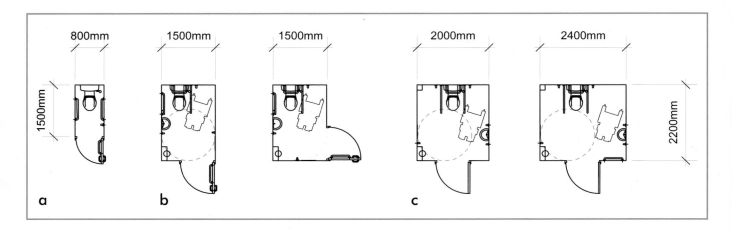

Plans and sections showing key dimensions around the wc pan in accessible toilets: for nursery and infant age children (a) and older primary and secondary age children (b). The dimensions given in Approved Document M (see regulations and guidance on page 125) are inappropriate for children.

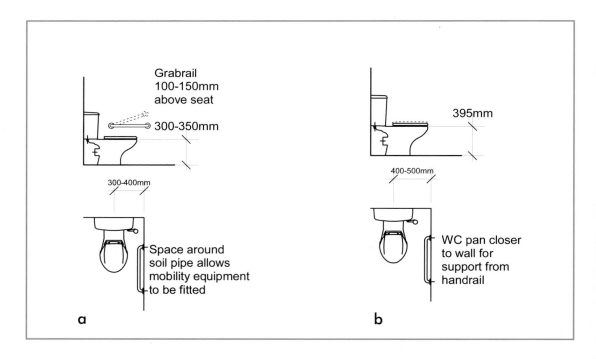

Plan showing a typical small toilet and shower of 6m² taken from Hampshire County Council's School Inclusion Design Brief (see page 125). This may be suitable for a mainstream school where some additional support is needed and it is often placed close to the main school entrance, where it can be used by visiting children and adults as well as school pupils.

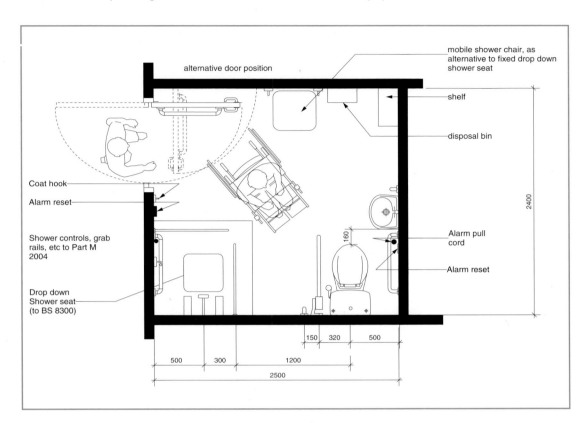

Hygiene rooms

Hygiene rooms need to provide a comfortable environment with a constant temperature (slightly higher than the rest of the school, see Heating and thermal comfort, page 151), with glare free lighting (uplighters may be suitable over the changing bed). The size of a hygiene room depends on the facilities provided. A space for assisted changing needs to be around 12–20m². Typical layouts are shown on pages 130–131. The following need to be provided in all cases:

• clinical wash-hand basins with lever taps for support staff, soap dispensers and hand drying facilities

• readily accessible storage for disposables, hand cream, alcohol wipes, plastic gloves, personal belongings, clean clothes

• panic alarms, suitably positioned to give adequate coverage (with a light and sounder in a manned area of the school for prompt assistance, and a suitably located reset button)

Baths or jacuzzi baths are not usually provided but if required there should be specific briefing for the designer and planned maintenance.

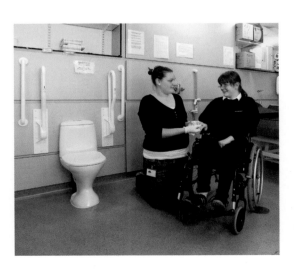

Hygiene rooms – examples of provision

The diagrams below and on the opposite page can be used as a guide. Reference should also be made to the regulations and guidance documents listed on page 125.

Plans showing cubicles for dry changing (a) and assisted toileting (b) .These may be used in early years and primary special schools. Portable hoists are shown. Ceiling mounted 'monotrack' hoists will not reach every part of a small changing room. 'X–Y' type hoists which cover the whole floor area may be suitable for larger changing rooms (with a ceiling height to suit).

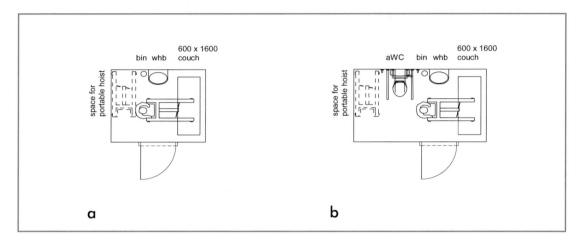

a   b

Plan showing a 12m² toilet/changing room with a peninsular wc and corner shower, taken from Hampshire County Council's School Inclusion Design Brief (see page 125). This would typically be used in an inclusive primary or secondary school.

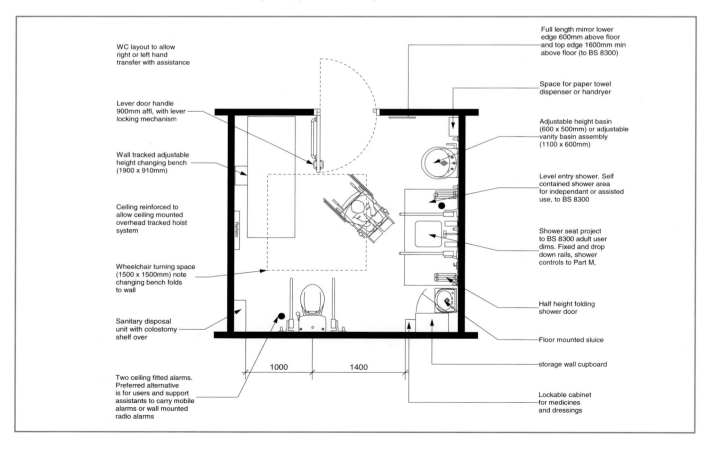

Alternative plans for larger toilet/changing room: peninsular changing trolley without wc (a) peninsular changing trolley with accessible wc, dual access (b) corner changing trolley (preferred by some staff) with accessible wc (c).

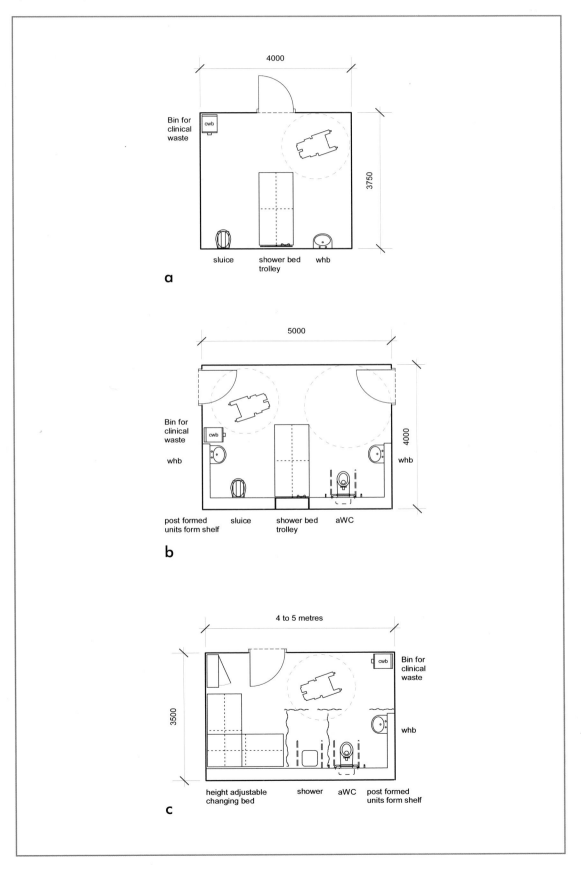

a

4000
3750
Bin for clinical waste
cwb
sluice shower bed trolley whb

b

5000
4000
Bin for clinical waste
cwb
whb
whb
post formed units form shelf sluice shower bed trolley aWC

c

4 to 5 metres
3500
cwb
Bin for clinical waste
whb
height adjustable changing bed shower aWC post formed units form shelf

Changing rooms

Changing rooms for PE or drama

For children aged 11 and above, changing accommodation, including showers, has to be provided (separate for boys and girls) for all children taking part in PE and school sports[44]. The facilities should be adjacent or close to the hall and within easy travelling distance to outside sports and activity areas.

For younger children, 'dry' changing areas are usually provided, and there may also need to be associated toilet and shower areas.

Children's changing rooms should be separate from those for staff and visitors.

An appropriate number of shower facilities should be available for ambulant and non-ambulant disabled users, with independent and/or assisted access.

The extent of wheelchair-accessible accommodation required and any space needed for visiting school teams and for community use needs to be established at the briefing stage. Wheelchair-accessible accommodation should be in close proximity to the hall and/or alongside other facilities[45].

44. Refer to:
The Education (School Premises) Regulations 1999 –
http://www.teachernet.gov.uk/sbregulatoryinformation/

45. Refer to:
Sport England's guidance note, Accessible Sports Facilities –
http://www.sportengland.org/facilities_guidance.htm

Changing rooms – key design points

- Good practice is for individual shower cubicles but some sports facilities may also have designated group shower areas.

- Stringent privacy may be required for some people because of individual needs or religious beliefs.

- The showers should have centrally controlled thermostatic water, with tamper-proof controls.

- There should be storage for dry and wet towels and arrangements made for their removal.

- Some disabled children prefer to use changing accommodation alongside their peers, so suitable accessible facilities should be provided within them, with sufficient circulation space throughout.

- Where there are likely to be only a few wheelchair users, self-contained, accessible toilet/changing rooms can be provided for use by boys or girls on different occasions.

- Accessible-assisted changing rooms have a peninsular toilet, a wheelchair accessible shower and/or a shower trolley and height adjustable changing bed. Flexibility for community use is possible if suitable access is made.

Changing rooms for hydrotherapy

Wet accessible changing areas are required for hydrotherapy, with access both from the school corridor and the pool area. Separate boys' and girls' facilities are provided for secondary age children and unisex/combined for primary age children.

Typically for a hydrotherapy pool there need to be changing facilities for:

• ambulant users, with a bench and hooks at the appropriate height

• independent users (or needing some support), with an accessible toilet, wash-hand basin, shower and ancillary facilities

• non-ambulant users, with a peninsular toilet, accessible wash-hand basin, shower and/or shower trolley, with a sluice and a height adjustable changing bed in a dry area, with suitable grab and guarding rails, shelves, bins, a store cupboard and plastic curtains for privacy

Two large hygiene spaces may provide for all these users as long as there is adequate privacy, depending on numbers of children and their needs. A larger provision might be needed for a warm water pool that may be used by more children at one time.

For more information on hydrotherapy pools, see Support spaces – Hydrotherapy, page 114, and Technical section – Warm water/hydrotherapy pools, page 156.

C

10e Kitchen facilities

Most schools prepare food on site but where this is not possible, schools have servery facilities for food delivered from elswhere.

Children with SEN and disabilities may have special dietary needs and food may sometimes need to be prepared for a variety of ways of consumption. In some instances, food preparation may need to be in a separate area. (Any such requirements should be stated in the brief.)

Area requirements

The size and type of catering accommodation will depend on the numbers taking school lunches and the type of catering chosen. Allowance should be made for other users, such as breakfast clubs, after-school clubs or community use.

Table 31 shows, as a guide, the area schedule for a kitchen and ancillary facilities at a special school of about 100 pupils and staff.

Key design issues

Specialist advice should be sought from the LA and specialist commercial kitchen designers, especially to ensure compliance with health, safety and food hygiene requirements, which are critical. The following covers the key design principles, with particular emphasis on health, safety and infection control[45].

45. Refer to: Inspirational Design for Kitchen and Dining Spaces – http://www.teachernet.gov.uk//sbdupublications/

Table 31: Typical special school of about 100 pupils – kitchen facilities	
Space	Area (m^2)
Kitchen	50
Servery	10
Office	6
Food store	6
Refuse store	6
Cleaners' store	2
Toilet/changing	4

Deliveries and waste disposal

There need to be:

• a designated place for regular deliveries, with easy access for delivery vehicles and the capability for catering staff to monitor delivery temperature, unpack and store food quickly

• safe disposal of refuse

• disposal of food waste separate from food preparation (rodent/pest proof)

• disposal of dirty linen and laundry separate from kitchen food preparation areas

• precautions to prevent ingress of insects, rodents and other pests into any food area

• a kitchen design that enables high standards of cleaning and disinfection to be maintained - all finishes will need to withstand regular cleaning and the impact of mechanical cleaning equipment, if used

Food preparation and storage

There should be:

- separation and handling of raw and cooked food and separation of clean and dirty activities, such as food preparation and dishwashing

- food preparation areas that are physically separate from the store for cleaning equipment and from sanitary facilities

- appropriate storage for food and other supplies

- adequate facilities for safe storage (at the correct temperature) of raw, fresh and cooked frozen food with cool rooms, larders, chilled stores, refrigerators and freezers

- storage of crockery and cutlery in a safe, clean environment

- linen storage in a hygienic location

Environmental design and services

There should be:

- sufficient ventilation to provide a comfortable environment for staff and prevent overheating - artificial ventilation should permit cleaning and maintenance

- dishwashers positioned to be accessible and capable of having the temperature checked (for thermostatic disinfection) if required

- a water supply and drainage for dealing with spillages - there should be adequate drains for the purpose (including accessible gullies and fat traps outside)

- an adequate number of wash-hand basins, with hot and cold water

Serving food

There should be:

- layouts that allow for prompt distribution of food trolleys from the kitchen area to serving areas

- serving arrangements that reflect the ages and height of all users, including wheelchair users, allowing them to collect their food and drink where self service is required – the counter design should have wheelchair knee space at various appropriate heights

Catering staff accommodation

Kitchen staff need a separate hygienic wheelchair accessible toilet and changing rooms adjacent to the kitchen, as well as a small office.

See Primary dining and Secondary dining, pages 66 and 99.

Detail development **D**

11
Technical

Building construction: elements, materials and finishes

Environmental services and sustainability

Warm water/hydrotherapy pools

Fire safety and evacuation

Furniture, fittings and equipment

Information and communication systems

This section provides key guidance on issues that affect children with SEN and disabilities and signposts to other documents for more detailed information.

11 Technical

This section looks at the technical detail relating to:

11a Building construction: elements, materials and finishes

- Ceilings, walls and floors
- Ramps, stairs and lifts
- Doors, windows and screens
- Wayfinding, signage and colour

11b Environmental services and sustainability

- Acoustics
- Lighting
- Heating and thermal comfort
- Ventilation
- Water services
- Medical gases
- Electrical services
- Environmental sustainability

11c Warm water/hydrotherapy pools

11d Fire safety and evacuation

11e Furniture, fittings and equipment

- Furniture
- Room layouts
- Furnishings and fittings
- Mobility needs and equipment

11f Information and communication systems (ICT)

11a Building construction: elements, materials and finishes

Specifying the detail in a building project is a crucial stage of the process. Children, young people and adults with SEN and disabilities are likely to be adversely affected if materials and construction details are poorly specified and installed.

This section offers general guidance on construction details. However, it is important to consult the LA or school's SEN specialists on a school's specific needs and to continue to check for accessibility and inclusion at every stage of design and construction. In many cases, good practice means providing a higher standard than the minimum legal requirement.

Key design issues

The inclusive design principles outlined in Part B apply to all aspects of building design and construction and need to be considered at the earliest stage. The following lists some key design issues, with more detailed guidance over the next few pages. These issues should not be addressed in isolation but as part of whole school strategies.

Robustness/durability – Take account of the likely deliberate or accidental damage, including the wear and tear caused by wheelchairs and other mobility equipment. Doors, architraves, external corners and the lower 300–450mm of walls are all areas of particular vulnerability. Choose materials that provide a robust finish to limit damage, or those that can easily be repaired and re-decorated.

Simplicity – Some children can become obsessive about details – keep things simple, with minimum changes of plane.

Safety – All building elements must be carefully assessed for safety – standard details might not be enough to protect children with SEN and disabilities, who may be particularly vulnerable. Avoid hard-edged corners or rough textures, for example.

Hygiene – Hygiene is a particular issue for the most vulnerable children. Avoid creating inaccessible places that cannot easily be cleaned. For instance, wide flat horizontal ledges can be a hiding place for dust and thrown rubbish.

Security – Balance the need for security with that for independence – when detailing doors and windows, for example.

Visual contrast – Provide visual contrast between surfaces and features to help with wayfinding and orientation. For example, between ceiling, wall and floor surfaces, between walls and doors, between door handles and the door's surface, and between sanitary fittings and walls. (See Wayfinding, page 147.)

D

1. Refer to:
Standard Specifications,
Layouts and Dimensions
(SSLD) 1: Partitions in
Schools –
http://www.teachernet.
gov.uk/management/
resourcesfinanceandbuild
ing/schoolbuildings/
innovativedesign/
standardspecifications/

Ceilings

Ceiling layouts will be needed to ensure coordination between tracking for hoists and other elements such as services, roof lights, and equipment such as projectors.

The following key issues should be considered:

• Where there is a risk of tampering or damage, such as toilets, indoor activity spaces or calming rooms, secure fixings will be needed (such as security clips to suspended ceiling tiles). Services should be concealed to avoid damage and interference.

• The structure must be able to support hoists and tracking in toilet/changing, physiotherapy spaces. Check with hoist manufacturers. (See Hoists, page 164.)

• Homogeneous ceilings with recessed light fittings may be needed in medical-treatment or 'clean areas'.

• Pool areas may need to allow for air movement above the ceiling to avoid mould growth.

• Sound-absorbent surfaces are required for most children with SEN, to ensure good sound quality. An acoustic consultant will need to advise on specialist spaces such as audiology suites. (See Acoustics, page 149.)

Ceiling mounted equipment may be used in a physiotherapy room.

Walls[1]

Drawing internal wall elevations is important because of the level of specialist equipment needed. It helps to ensure that fixtures and services are fully coordinated with fixed furniture, fittings and equipment.

The following key issues should be considered:

• Sliding folding partitions between spaces can increase flexibility but it may be difficult to provide enough sound insulation, especially for children with hearing impairment.

• Walls may need to support heavy equipment and the force of a child pulling on equipment (for example, wall bars in a physiotherapy room, grab rails in toilets). Where lightweight construction is used, additional framing supports and impact-resistant boards may be needed.

• Walls need to be easy to repair if there is any accidental or deliberate damage. Exposed corners may need to be protected. Dado rails and handrails offer protection both to the wall and the children, but need to be carefully detailed near openings and in relation to services, fixtures and fittings.

• Smooth, cleanable, relatively impermeable surfaces will help infection control. Full tiling is needed in hygiene areas, kitchens and toilets.

• Smooth non-abrasive materials are less likely to cause harm if a child falls or brushes against the wall, if there is boisterous behaviour, or if accidents occur. In some spaces (for example calming rooms), walls need to be clad with smooth but firm, impact-resistant, non-abrasive materials or linings, to reduce risk that a child can self-harm.

• The construction of partitions and absorbency of wall surfaces needs to take account of the needs of people with hearing impairment.
(See Acoustics, page 149.)

Floors[2]

The following key issues should be considered in the design and specification of floor finishes:

• Specifications should take account of wheelchair use. Any wheelchair tracking should be planned at the start.

• Floors should be smooth and slip resistant in both dry and wet situations. (The slip coefficients of adjacent floor finishes need to be similar.) Trip hazards need to be avoided and changes in level clearly identified. (See Ramps and Steps and stairs, page 142–3.) The risk of particularly vulnerable children falling and being hurt should be assessed.

• Floors should be easy to maintain, impact resistant, and hard wearing – particularly in view of the likelihood of children soiling them. Taking advice from manufacturers should ensure fitness for purpose and guaranteed cleaning regimes.

• Changes in colour may be used for wayfinding, although highly polished or patterned floors are confusing for people with visual impairment. (See Wayfinding, page 147.)

• A sound-absorbing surface or backing is important for people with sensory impairment or who are noise sensitive. If hard surfaces are used, such as woodblock or timber floors, then additional consideration will need to be given to sound attenuation on other surfaces.

• There needs to be a balance between softness and strength, taking account of the use of mobility equipment. Well-insulated backgrounds, which help with maintaining comfortable conditions and are warm underfoot, are especially useful where very young children or those with mobility needs use the floor.

The choice of finish will vary according to activities and children's needs but the following is a general guide:

• Carpet is soft, acoustically absorbent and can be calming but a type should be specified which does not cause friction burns to children who use the floor. Carpet is also more difficult to clean. To prevent dirt and dust build ups, which can affect people with allergies, carpet tiles may be overlaid on sheet flooring, if safely secured. Carpet is not advisable where there is heavy traffic, spillage or soiling. It may not be suitable for children who might be affected by the dust that can accumulate in a carpet.

• Slip resistant sheet flooring with acoustic backing (such as linoleum) is hygienic, water-resistant and suitable for use in wet areas near sinks and where soiling and sickness are likely to occur.

• Ceramic tiles are suitable for wet areas such as showers and hydrotherapy pools. They need careful specification for slip-resistance, especially for ramps and changes in level[3].

2. Refer to: Standard Specifications, Layouts and Dimensions (SSLD) 2: Floor Finishes in Schools – http://www.teachernet. gov.uk/management/ resourcesfinanceandbuild ing/schoolbuildings/ innovativedesign/ standardspecifications/

3. Refer to: BS 8300 Design of buildings and their approaches to meet the needs of disabled people – http://www.bsi-global. com/shop

D

Table 32: Key dimentions for internal and external ramps

Clear width (between walls/upstands)

1200mm minimum –1800mm preferred
(1500mm minimum in Approved Document M)

Gradient

1 in 12 for 2m length	(166mm max rise)
1 in 15 for 5m length	(333mm max rise)
1 in 20 for 10m length	(500mm max rise)

Landings

1200mm long at foot and head, 1500mm long at intermediate landings

Intermediate landings of 1800x1800mm should be provided as passing places when it is not possible for a wheelchair user to see from one end of the ramp to the other, or the ramp has three flights or more.

NB These are minimum dimensions, clear of any door swing or obstruction.

4. Refer to:
The Building Regulations, Approved Document M –
http://
www.planningportal.gov.uk/buildingregulations
and
BS 8300: Design of buildings and their approaches to meet the needs of disabled people –
http://www.bsi-global.com/shop

Internal and external ramps[4]

- Gradients should be as shallow as practicable, as steep gradients create difficulties for some wheelchair users who lack the strength to propel themselves up a slope, or have difficulty in slowing down or stopping.

- Some children who can walk but have restricted mobility can find it more difficult to negotiate a ramp rather than a short stair, so a choice of routes should be provided.

- Approved Document M notes that ramps have a surface width of 1500mm between walls. Wider ramps should be considered where there is likely to be a high proportion of disabled users.

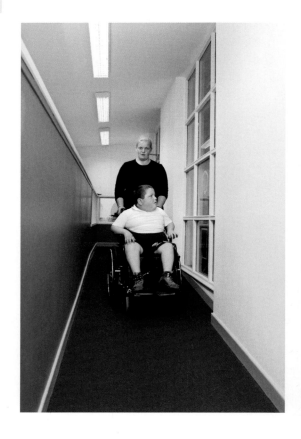

Steps and stairs[5]

The following should be considered:

• The minimum clear width permitted by Approved Document M is 1200mm but this is only advisable in schools for little used stairs. Standard Specifications, Layouts and Dimensions (SSLD) 6 recommends a clear width of 1600mm, which enables two adults to pass each other with ease and permits three people to safely carry down a wheelchair.

• There should be visual contrast between stair nosings and the treads and risers. For external steps, tactile information should be provided, such as corduroy tactile paving to the top and bottom of the steps.

• There should be safe protected refuges of a suitable size on all staircases for evacuation, with appropriate communication links.

• Additional low handrails should be provided for children under 12.

Table 33: Key dimensions for steps and stairs
Rise
150mm–170mm (150mm preferred for schools)
Going
250mm minimum (280mm preferred for schools)
Clear width between handrails
1200mm minimum (1600mm preferred)
Handrails
To both sides, extending 300mm past the top and bottom of each flight. For children under 12, 40mm–45mm diameter, at a height of 600mm from the pitch line of the stair or ground level.
Landings
1200mm long minimum

5. Refer to:
Standard Specifications, Layouts and Dimensions (SSLD) 6: Internal Stairways in Schools – http://www.teachernet. gov.uk/management/ resourcesfinanceandbuild ing/schoolbuildings/ innovativedesign/ standardspecifications/

The Building Regulations, Approved Document M 2004 sections 1 & 3 – http:// www.planningportal.gov. uk/buildingregulations

Building Bulletin 100 – Design for Fire Safety in Schools – http://www.teachernet. gov.uk/sbdupublications/

The Building Regulations Approved Document B Volume 2 – http:// www.planningportal.gov. uk/buildingregulations

D

7. Refer to
The Building Regulations
Approved Document M –
http://
www.planningportal.gov.
uk/buildingregulations
and
BS 8300 –
http://www.bsi-global.
com/shop
Both give guidance on
accessible controls,
tactile signs and symbols.

8. Platform lifts can
be used if no other
suitable alternative
means is available, but
they should not reduce
the effective width of
corridors or stairs.
Refer to:
BS 6440 Powered lifting
platforms for use by
disabled persons. Code
of practice –
http://www.bsi-global.
com/shop

Lifts[7]

Lifts are essential for vertical circulation for wheelchair users[8]. In order to calculate the number, size and location of lifts, the following need to be taken into account:

• The number of children, staff and visitors expected

• How many are going to be using wheelchairs and other aids, the size of these aids and how many will need assistance alongside

• The density and frequency of use, including for the peak times of use – a flow analysis should assess peak change over times. An appropriate speed, size and waiting time should be identified. The minimum waiting time should be at least 'good' as defined by CIBSE

• The maintenance strategy – i.e. action in the eventuality of breakdowns and repairs

Table 34: Key standards for lifts
Approved Document M
Minimum lift size to all storeys gives access for a wheelchair user and a support worker (evacuation standard): 1100 x 1400mm with 900mm wide door. This may be suitable for a primary school.
BS 8300
Minimum lift size:1400mm x 2000mm with 1100mm wide door. This may be suitable for a secondary school. Wheelchair user can turn 180 degrees and can include another wheelchair user or person with mobility aids.
BS 5588 Pt 5 & 8
Suggests one evacuation lift for each designated evacuation staircase.

9. Refer to:
BS 5588-8:1999
Fire precautions in the
design, construction and use
of buildings. Code of practice
for means of escape for
disabled people –
http://www.bsi-global.
com/shop

• The arrangements for using lifts – whether they will be available to all occupants or restricted to disabled people (e.g. with a close proximity fob or key operation)

Lifts should be large enough for a wheelchair user (or users if there are likely to be several) to enter and leave the lift independently or assisted by a support worker alongside as appropriate. Significantly larger size lifts are essential for groups of pupils in wheelchairs moving around alongside their peers.

Evacuation lifts are necessary for multi-level schools. (See Fire safety and evacuation, page 158.)

Lifts should be well lit and user friendly, without looking purpose designed for disabled users. The following should be provided:

• Lift doors (with visual contrast to the surrounding wall) that are wide enough and operate slowly enough to allow people in wheelchairs to enter and exit the lift safely

• A mirror – positioned to help children and adults who cannot turn their wheelchairs around – to reverse out of the lift, and a handrail

• Suitable signage, accessible controls at the correct height, speech announcements, visual and tactile indicators, visual and audible alarms, and an emergency communication system with an induction loop[9]

Doors and door openings[10]

In some settings, it will be necessary to provide doors to a higher standard than that required by current regulations to ensure robustness, particularly where there are significant numbers of children using wheelchairs.

Doors need to meet the requirements for accessibility, means of escape, safety and security. Any conflicting needs will have to be resolved. For example, Building Regulations Approved Document B Part 2 requires that fire doors have a maximum opening pressure of 30N but this makes it difficult for some children with disabilities to open them. Therefore in this case doors on corridors should be held open on electro-magnetic hold back devices that will hold the door open until the fire alarm is activated. The school must develop an evacuation plan because in the event of a fire many of the disabled occupants will be unable to operate the doors without assistance. (See Fire safety and evacuation, page 158.)

All openings and doors must be wide enough to give easy access to everyone, including disabled people.

Complying with the Building Regulations Approved Document M (Table 2, minimum effective clear width of doors) and BS 8300 (Table 2 - 6.4.1) will be appropriate for many disabled adults (i.e. independent wheelchair users with upper body mobility and strength). But it is important to consider the evolving capabilities of disabled children.

The following factors need to be considered:

• The type and size of any mobility aid used (frames, sticks, walkers and wheelchairs, and in special schools side-lying trolleys and standing frames)

• Whether children use wheelchairs independently or are assisted by support workers (See Mobility needs and equipment, page 164.)

When specifying doors, the capability of the user (for example, dexterity, strength, visual acuity) needs to be borne in mind. Doors should:

• be easy to identify and user friendly to operate

• allow good visibility on both sides of the door for all users, to create an inclusive, welcoming environment

• have the appropriate strength, impact-resistance and durability, robustness and integrity

• provide the appropriate sound insulation properties

• be smooth and easily cleaned and maintained (Laminate finishes can provide colour and visual contrast.)

External doors and thresholds

All external doors should be easy to operate or automatic (preferably sliding). Main entrance doors should be operated automatically by sensors/push button or other means.

External doors should have level thresholds to a well-drained, safe external area. Where thresholds are

10. Refer to:
Building Bulletin 100 – Design for Fire Safety in Schools – http://www.teachernet. gov.uk/sbdupublications/

The Building Regulations, Approved Document M sections 1& 3 cover minimum width of openings for different situations – http:// www.planningportal.gov. uk/buildingregulations

Standard Specifications, Layouts and Dimensions (SSLD) 7: Internal Doorsets in Schools – http://www.teachernet. gov.uk/management/ resourcesfinanceandbuild ing/schoolbuildings/ innovativedesign/ standardspecifications/ and
BS 8300: Design of buildings and their approaches to meet the needs of disabled people – http://www.bsi-global. com/shop

BS EN 1935:2002 Building hardware. Single-axis hinges. Requirements and test methods – http://www.bsi-global. com/shop

D

used, they should comply with Approved Document M and BS 8300.

A firm flush mat is required to avoid trip hazards and reduce wet floor surfaces.

Internal doors

Manoeuvring large heavy doors can be problematic. It may be necessary to limit the need for door closers. Hinges should be selected for heavy use along with doors and frames as described in BS EN 1935:2002. (See note 10, page 145.) The minimum clear opening width required by Approved Document M is 800mm. In some special schools a wider opening may help those who need more assistance. Usually, a clear door opening width of 900mm on a corridor width of 1500mm–1800mm (preferably 2000mm–3000mm) allows access for a range of wheelchair users. Where there is a narrow corridor (under 1500mm wide), or larger wheelchairs or equipment, an extra side door leaf or a clear opening width of 1000–1100mm can be provided.

Vision panels between 500mm and 1500mm high with safety glass should be provided in doors for visibility and supervision, except where security is required. Blinds can provide privacy. Manifestations may also be required.

Ironmongery should be smooth, easily cleaned, safe and convenient to use. Designers also need to consider the following:

- Safety – anti-finger-trap, if properly maintained, are helpful for small children and children at risk. Double action hinges and a removable stop (usually provided as standard) allow toilet doors to be opened outwards in an emergency.
- Accessibility/ergonomics – the mounting height and shape should allow all users to control the handle, including those with limited dexterity and/or strength. A clear mode of operation is needed (such as push and pull) for children learning to use doors.
- Access control – may be needed, for example for when children run out and there is risk of harm. Designers should discuss the needs with staff.
- Electronic door entry system – need to ensure that all users, including those with visual or hearing impairments and wheelchair users, could operate it.
- Deep kick-plates and door frame protectors – help to prevent damage by wheelchairs.
- Door seals (as fitted for smoke control or sound insulation) – these affect the closing pressures required by Approved Document M and BS 8300. It may not therefore be possible to meet the fire and acoustic requirements as well as the closing pressure requirements in all situations.

Windows and screens

Internal glazed screens can be used to provide borrowed light and enable passive supervision by teachers. They also let children see what is happening and not feel enclosed. Blinds may be required to avoid distraction, or to give privacy. Manifestation is needed to glazing. Glazed screens should provide the sound reduction required in Building Bulletin 93.

Low-level windows with safety glazing allow very young children and children lying down to have a view out. However, some children can be distracted by views to the outside and activities taking place.

All fittings need to be tamper proof and prevent children from climbing out if they are distressed.

See also Lighting, page 149, Acoustics, page 149 and Ventilation, page 152.

The width of opening required depends on the width and angle of approach.

Wayfinding and signage[11]

Wayfinding and signage are invaluable for people with a range of SEN and disabilities such as sensory impairments, speech, communication and language needs or learning disability.

Colour, texture, acoustics, lighting and sound, as well as landmark features such as seating or plants, can all help people orientate themselves on their journey around the school. Views to the outside and through to other parts of the building and site can also help people find their way. People with a visual impairment may recognise where they are because noise levels, smells and other non-visual signals reflect the character of a space.

Wayfinding schemes can be created, enhanced by well designed and carefully placed signage. For example:

• defining routes through large open areas with contrasting textures or floor finishes

• defining routes with contrasting colour or tone on walls

• using voice signals which react to movement or other triggers

• placing signs at junctions or in long passageways to indicate direction or position

Signage should:

• be clear and easily understood – simple symbols, used consistently, may be more appropriate than letters in some cases

• be well lit and carefully sited

• make clear distinctions between signs that offer directions and those that indicate arrival

• be located so that everyone can see it, including people in wheelchairs – it may be better to fix signs lower rather than higher

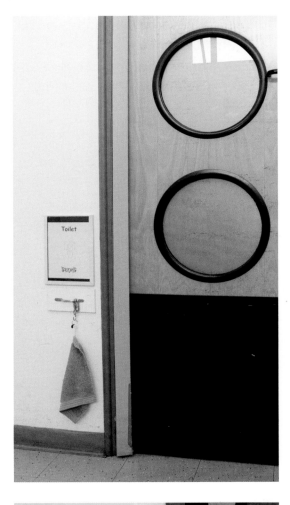

Glazed door panels at different heights help people to orientate themselves and enable them to see if anyone is approaching from the other side.

11. Refer to: The Sign Design Guide published jointly by JMU Access Partnership and the Sign Design Society – http://www.signdesignsociety.co.uk/

Signs should be easy to understand. Words, symbols and objects can all be used.

D

12. Refer to:
Building Regulations
Approved Document M –
http://
www.planningportal.gov.
uk/buildingregulations
and
BS 8300: Design of
buildings and their
approaches to meet
the needs of disabled
people –
http://www.bsi-global.
com/shop
and
Colour and Contrast:
Design guidance for
internal built environ-
ments, from ICI Dulux
and Keith Bright et al
University of Reading –
www.duluxtrade.co.uk
and
Disability: Making
Buildings Accessible,
Keith Bright –
www.workplacelaw.net

Changes in texture,
shape and colour
can all help
people to orientate
themselves.

• have visual (i.e. tonal) contrast to its background[12] (See Colour, below.)

• have lettering of appropriate size and shape, using serif-free text, upper and lower case lettering and contrasting colours

• provide embossed tactile lettering, incorporating Braille where required or other tactile information, for instance on classroom doors

• avoid bright or shiny surfaces that can be distracting

Colour

Colour should be considered in relation to light levels, visibility, maintenance and psychological effect. The following points may be useful:

• A bright surface against a dark background can be glaring and reduce visibility (such as a window in a dark wall or frame).

• Bright colour in large areas, or busy patterns, can confuse or over-stimulate.

• Some patterns can produce a strobe effect and should be avoided.

• Pastel subdued colours can be soothing.

• Layering colour will define objects for some visually impaired people. Remember, however, that some people are colour blind (particularly between red and green).

• Colour on architectural features is useful for signalling a change in activity.

• Colour coding can identify spaces.

• Colour or tonal contrast can be used to identify objects such as light switches against a wall or utensils or tools on work surfaces or possible hazards such as step edges.

Research suggests that the ability of visually impaired people to identify differences in colour is strongly correlated to the amount of light that the coloured surface reflects.

Photo Andrew Lee

11b Environmental services[13] and sustainability

Environmental services are particularly important for the comfort and well-being of children with SEN and disabilities. Some children may be more sensitive to light, for example, or need high levels of sound insulation.

This section sets out the main considerations that apply to children with special needs and disabilities.

Acoustics

Many children with SEN and disabilities have a particular reliance on good room acoustics and sound insulation – between rooms and from outside noise – for their access to learning. Poor acoustic conditions, such as noise distraction and high ambient noise levels, are particularly unacceptable where there are children with sensory impairments and/or communication difficulties (for example in a designated unit or special school). However, it is worth noting that special schools generally have lower occupancy and background noise than mainstream schools.

Rooms with long reverberation times, with surfaces that are acoustically highly reflective (i.e. those with large volumes and hard dense surfaces), are particularly unsuitable for many types of children's needs - some children with autism, for example, would find the room distressing. Children with a hearing impairment can also find the noise painful because it is amplified by their hearing aids.

NB Acoustic calculations for all learning and teaching spaces are now required to demonstrate compliance with Part F of the Building Regulations.

Many special schools have children with hearing impairment or sensitive hearing. In these cases, specialist advice will be needed from acousticians, audiologists specialising in hearing impairment, teachers of the deaf, and/or other specialists. Specialist provision may include personal hearing aids and radio aids in conjunction with induction loops and sound-field systems as described in Table 6.2 of Building Bulletin 93[14].

Where a special school is co-located with a mainstream school, the acoustic performance of shared spaces in the mainstream school must also be considered to ensure effective inclusion.

Specialist advice can be obtained from:

- the Institute of Acoustics www.ioa.org.uk
- the National Deaf Children's Society www.ndcs.org.uk
- the Royal National Institute for the Deaf www.rnid.org.uk
- audiologists

Lighting[15]

Lighting must take into account the different needs of children with SEN and disabilities. Children with impaired vision, for example, need lighting levels that enhance their sight. Those with hearing impairment need clear visibility for lipreading and signing, for orientation and using signage and wayfinding. Safety is a key factor: poor visibility and poor surface contrast may contribute to accidents. Input from a lighting specialist is recommended where there are complex visual needs.

A school's orientation and any natural shading on the site should be considered at the outset, including the location of spaces that generate the most heat, and the need for and detailing of shading devices. The Royal National Institute for the Blind (RNIB) or similar organisations can advise on specialist environments for children with visual or multiple impairments.

13. The environmental criteria for schools are addressed in various Building Bulletins and other publications. Building Bulletin 87 – Guidelines for Environmental Design in Schools - http://teachernet.gov.uk/energy provides general guidance. Other guides are listed below.

14. The standards in BB93 Acoustic Design of Schools – http://teachernet.gov.uk/acoustics recommend good quality acoustics for a general learning environment.

Where there are specialist areas for children with hearing impairment, refer to Section 6 of Building Bulletin 93, which addresses the particular needs of children with hearing impairments. The case studies in Section 7 of Building Bulletin 93 include examples of specialist provision for deaf and hearing impaired children. Appendix 8 – specifications for sound-field systems – includes requirements for loudspeakers, microphones and sound amplification.

15. Building Bulletin 90 Lighting Design for Schools (superseded by CIBSE LG5 in 2008) provides general guidance on lighting in schools – http://teachernet.gov.uk/lighting

D

Designs should avoid glare, silhouetting, reflections, shadows and any other interference that causes visual confusion. For instance, a teacher's or child's face could be in shadow against a window or bright or highly reflective surfaces, or have shadows cast by electric lighting. Good tonal contrast is important.

There will be times when teachers will want to change the mood of a space to create a more calming or stimulating environment. Window blinds and electric dimming can help with this, as can local controls.

Daylighting

Daylighting is important for all schools, and children with limited mobility in particular benefit from a connection to the outdoors and a view out. However, some pupils with SEN may be particularly sensitive to glare from direct or reflected sunlight, so it is important to be able to control light entering the space. (See Curtains and blinds, page 164.)

The window wall should be light in colour. A brightly lit outdoor view through a window can be glaring against a dark wall - a particular hazard at the end of a corridor.

A minimum average daylight factor of 2 per cent is considered adequate for most areas in mainstream schools. However, the optimum of 4–5 per cent minimum average daylight factor (on the working plane) may be preferable for schools with children with SEN and disabilities, provided that an acceptable uniformity ratio can be maintained, avoiding under-lit areas furthest from windows. This applies to learning, circulation and assembly spaces. In deep spaces lit by windows in one wall only, ceilings may need to be higher than average with high levels of light reflectance to achieve a 4–5 per cent minimum average daylight factor. Where there is a number of children with visual impairment or sensitivity to light, or where there are conflicting needs, specialist lighting advice may be needed.

Electric lighting

Light fittings should be low glare, avoiding any flicker and unwanted noise.

It may be necessary to avoid visible light sources – over changing beds or therapy couches, for example. Uplighters may be more suitable for some children with autism.

Automatic sensors that switch off lighting when no movement is detected may not be suitable for children who are less mobile. Switches may be useful in teaching children how to use them.

Heating and thermal comfort

Thermal comfort is governed by air temperature, the radiant temperature, humidity and air movement, and varies according to children's special needs. Table 35 suggests design air temperatures for a variety of environments. If children are non-ambulant, or have low activity rates, the design temperature may need to be slightly higher than otherwise.

Extremes of temperature cause discomfort, particularly for children with SEN and disabilities, who may be more sensitive and have complex health needs. This can be distressing for them, especially if they cannot communicate their discomfort. Teachers and carers should be able to respond to this through adjustable tamper-proof local controls, such as thermostatic radiator valves and individual room controls, in any space that is used for more than a transitory period. Localised supplementary heating and cooling may also be required in some cases. Measures to control heat gains, such as shading devices for solar control, should therefore be provided.

NB Specialist equipment can also raise the temperature of a space.

Buildings with exposed thermal mass combined with night cooling and/or ground-coupled ventilation may help to keep internal temperatures stable.

Heating systems

For **standard radiators** a surface temperature of 60–70 degrees C is commonly used in schools. A risk assessment is necessary for children with SEN. For example, some children should only be exposed to low surface temperatures.

Low surface temperature radiators (~43 degrees C and not greater than 46 degrees C) are used where there are very young children, children with severe and profound learning difficulties or complex health needs.

Low temperature heating systems, such as **underfloor heating**, may be suitable in a special school. They are less prone to overheating but tend to have slow response times. Where there is a risk of sudden heat loss – for example when doors are opened – then supplementary heating may be required. A surface temperature of 26 degrees ± 2 degrees C, the comfort temperature for low activity, should not be exceeded where children are sitting. Underfloor heating may not be suitable where large areas are covered with mats (used for some activities with children with special needs) or where regular spillages occur (for hygiene and odour control).

Table 35: Ambient design temperatures in schools
18°C–21°C
This temperature is in line with conditions required by mainstream schools. Pupils are normally clothed, ambulant and reasonably active, even if sedentary at work.
23°C
This applies to special schools and resourced provision, where needs of pupils tend to be complex and varied, including pupils with physical difficulties or profound and multiple learning difficulties.
25°C–30°C
Where children may be wet or partially clothed for a significant length of time, rapidity of air movement can lead to chilling by evaporation. To compensate, a higher design temperature may be required. In areas used for medical inspection, bathing and changing, the air speed in these environments should not exceed 0.1 ms−1 at 25°C.
28°C
In mainstream schools, when this temperature is reached or exceeded, overheating is said to occur. But children whose special needs mean they are more sensitive to high temperatures may overheat at a lower temperature. Measures should be taken at the design stage as a priority, to ensure the sensitivities of pupils are considered.

D

16. For general guidance refer to Building Bulletin 101 – Ventilation of School Buildings – http://teachernet.gov.uk/iaq

Fan convectors can be a source of background noise, circulate dust and contaminants, and lead to cross infection.

Radiant ceiling panels have high surface temperature and can create thermal stratification, so tall people may feel hot around head height and children who spend some time on the floor may not have enough heat.

NB To minimise the collection of dust and pathogens that can be a source of infection to vulnerable pupils, all heated surfaces should be smooth, easy to clean, accessible and robust. Low-level boxing and exposed pipe-work should be avoided wherever possible.

Ventilation[16]

Effective ventilation, with adequate fresh air, is important in all schools. Stale air with high levels of carbon dioxide affects concentration and can cause drowsiness. This effect may be more pronounced in children with special needs.

For schools where there are children with complex health needs, ventilation systems can be a potential source of contamination, and may need to be designed for infection control or to maintain standards of hygiene.

Table 36 gives recommended air changes for specialist spaces in schools. Rates for other areas found in mainstream schools are given in Building Bulletin 101.

Ventilation systems may be natural, mechanical or mixed mode. Energy demand can be reduced by minimising the use of air conditioning and recovering heat from mechanical ventilation systems.

Table 36: Recommended air changes in specialist spaces
Laundries, soiled holding or waste, cleaners' rooms
5 air changes per hour minimum Mechanical extract with natural or mechanical make-up air, as appropriate
Toilet and changing spaces
10 air changes per hour minimum Mechanical extract to outside make-up air, heated and filtered
Physiotherapy, medical and sick rooms
8 litres per second or between 2 and 2.5 air changes per hour minimum when occupied

Natural ventilation

- Staff should be able to control ventilation for comfort, and draughts should be minimised around vulnerable and immobile pupils.

- Ventilation design should not compromise acoustic performance, since children with SEN may have additional sensitivities to external sources of noise. It is essential that operating mechanisms are designed to be virtually silent, as operation during lessons is very distracting. Some automatic window/rooflight opening systems, for instance, can make a noise.

Mechanical ventilation

- Rapid extract ventilation, as well as opening windows, may be used to remove smells, fumes, heat or dust from kitchens, practical spaces, medical, therapy, toilet or changing spaces. Supply inlets should always be positioned to draw in clean air, avoiding extract outlets that risk recirculation.

- COSHH regulations require most practical areas to be fitted with some form of local dust and/or fume extraction from woodworking machinery or where certain adhesives are used. This can be particularly important where there are children with breathing difficulties, such as asthma.

Infection control

- Mechanical ventilation can transmit infection via pathogens in the air, dust and droplets that evaporate, or via a common vehicle such as shoes or wheelchairs, as can recirculating air systems.

- However, in some cases, mechanical ventilation may be required for hygiene and infection control for vulnerable children and young people with complex health needs. It may require filtration to grades F4 or F6, depending on external air quality and design exposure levels for the protection of pupils.

- Toilets, showers, changing areas, laundries, cleaners' rooms and spaces holding soiled clothes or clinical waste should be mechanically ventilated to be slightly negatively pressurised relative to adjacent spaces.

- Good access is essential for maintaining ventilation systems and ductwork to avoid the risk of infection. (Pre-filters will increase the life of main filters.)

- Children with SEN may be more vulnerable to bacteria found in cooling towers and moisture in duct work.

D

17. Building Bulletin 87 – Guidelines for Environmental Design in Schools provides general guidance on hot and cold water in schools – http://www.teachernet.gov.uk/sbdupublications/

CIRIA's guidance (W012) on sustainable water management in schools covers sustainable water management and drainage strategies, which are an important aspect in the sustainable design of schools – http://www.ciria.org/suds/publications.htm

18. Refer to:
The Control of Legionella Bacteria in Water Systems (L8). Approved Code of Practice and guidance, ISBN 0717617726 – http://www.hse.gov.uk/legionnaires/.

19. Specialist advice must be sought on the use and storage of medical gas cylinders.

20. Refer to:
The Building Regulations Approved Document B – http://www.planningportal.gov.uk/buildingregulations and
BS 4163 – Health and safety for design and technology in schools and similar establishments – http://www.bsi-global.com/shop

Water services[17]

All hot water delivered at outlets such as basins, sinks and showers used by vulnerable pupils should be at a low temperature (~43°C and not greater than 46°C). This should be achieved through the use of local fail-safe thermostatic mixing valves.

More water storage may be required in special schools because of higher usage, particularly for children with complex health needs.

Guidance in 'L8', HSE's code of practice for the control of legionella bacteria in water systems, should be followed[18].

NB The vulnerability of some children with SEN and disabilities to infection should be borne in mind when the site surface water and foul drainage systems are designed.

Medical gases[19]

Some children with complex health needs are oxygen dependant. A medical gas cylinder store may be needed close to its point of use and with clear access for delivery. The store should be clearly marked, well ventilated, lockable and not vulnerable to vandalism. Cylinder stores should ideally be located at ground level, not underground (for example in a basement) and as close as possible to the delivery point. Doors should open outwards.

Electrical services

There may be a greater requirement for electrical services to support children with SEN and disabilities in schools. Specialist systems include a range of specialist equipment in multi-sensory rooms. Safety measures should ensure that all children are made aware of risks or hazards – in practical areas, science laboratories or design and technology workshops, for example, where there is a risk of hair being trapped in machinery. Visual and audible warning can be used to indicate safe working and emergency stop buttons will isolate electrical supply[20]. See also Information and communication systems, page 167, Lifts, page 144, and Fire safety and evacuation, page 158.

Environmental sustainability

Promoting sustainable development can be an integral part of the learning experience for the whole school. Many special schools make exemplary use of their external landscape for learning and teaching.

As for all schools, designs should minimise the adverse environmental effect of pollutants, reduce carbon emissions and waste, recycle materials, and encourage biodiversity. However, in some special schools the following issues may have a significant impact on the approach for sustainable design:

- Transport of children with SEN and disabilities to and from school - providing vehicular access and car parking for them, staff and visitors
- Higher water use needed for healthcare, laundry and hydrotherapy
- Higher internal temperatures, maintaining steady state ambient conditions
- The provision of thermal mass to reduce diurnal temperature variations
- More extensive mechanical ventilation and cooling for health and infection control
- Hydrotherapy pool installations
- The greater use of technology
- The use of automated systems - access and door controls, fire safety, security, communications, hoists and mobility equipment
- Handling and disposal of materials and waste
- Safe use and storage of medicines and medical gas cylinders

BREEAM

The DCSF's specific requirements for environmental sustainability within its capital programmes are that all new school buildings and refurbishment projects above a threshold[21] achieve at least a 'very good' rating using BREEAM Schools (the Building Research Establishment's Environmental Assessment Method), and that all new school buildings meet the reduction in carbon emissions set out on the Teachernet website[22]. Schools catering for a high level of children with SEN and disabilities will find it more difficult than mainstream schools. However, BREEAM Schools can be applied to most special schools using the same criteria as other schools, and the requirement applies in most cases[23].

For children with acute SEN there are particular requirements that may reduce opportunities to achieve BREEAM credits. These include options to naturally ventilate parts of a school, and some of the transport credits, such as cyclist facilities. In these cases the Bespoke BREEAM version may be used.

Carbon emissions

DCSF has set a target on carbon emissions for all new school buildings of at least 60 per cent below those predicted for a notional building as set out in Approved Document L2A. Compliance with this requirement can be demonstrated through the use of a Carbon Calculator, which the DCSF has developed, and which is available from Teachernet[24].

In recognition of the fact that the energy used within a school catering for children with SEN is dependant on the type of need, and that this may be significantly higher than in mainstream schools, the Carbon Calculator contains a worksheet which lists its underlying assumptions and allows users to alter these assumptions accordingly.

21. £500,000 for primary schools and £2 million for secondary schools and involving rebuilding or complete refurbishment of more than 10% of the floor area of a school

22. Refer to: www.teachernet.gov.uk \carbontargets

23. Refer to: BREEAM Schools web page – http://www.breeam.org /schools

24. See note 22 above.

D

11c Warm water/ hydrotherapy pools

The Support section of this book gives general guidance on hydrotherapy pools, including the area required.

Pools are costly to install and maintain, so it is especially important that sufficient funding is secured at the outset. Specialist design advice must also be sought so that health and safety requirements are met, and to help ensure an energy efficient solution and economic running costs.

Pools are usually designed and installed by specialists, who should be carefully selected for their previous reliable performance and the guarantees or warranties available.

Hydrotherapy pools are used by vulnerable people and must be safe and accessible. Health and safety considerations and infection control are paramount and the following should be considered:

• Clear sightlines for supervision and safety

• Sufficient space for the number of adults responsible for supervision

• An alarm system so that staff can summon assistance

• Specification of finishes and detailed design of the pool (Specialist technical advice will be required.)

• The profile of the pool floor, which should allow for any change of water depth to be gradual (In small swimming pools this may be difficult to achieve.)

Access

All pools need accessible changing, toilet and showering facilities (including pool-side showers) for independent or assisted use, and accessible wet changing areas must be provided adjacent to the pool. See Changing rooms for hydrotherapy, page 133.

The pool edge should be colour contrasted with the pool water/tank, to enable the edge to be seen clearly by pool users, both in the water and on the pool surround.

There should be one or two hoists for independent or assisted access to the pool. Sometimes a ceiling-mounted hoist direct from the changing areas can be provided but the length of travel must not compromise treating individuals with dignity and respect.

The pool surround should be wide enough to accommodate the hoist and for safe circulation. The following should be considered:

• The rationale for whether the pool is to be raised, level-deck or sunken

• Ease of access and supervision requirements in terms of health and safety

• Whether the water level is to be at or below floor level with a ramped access, or above and contained within a raised broad surround wide enough to support a child or young person being transferred into the water by staff and 'floated' into or out of the water (avoiding the need to be lifted)

There should be a ramp and shallow steps with handrails into the water.

Light and sound

Specialist advice should be sought early on about sensory equipment, lighting and sound, along with underwater lighting features (which require specialist installation to ensure safety). Lighting should be positioned to avoid problems created by flickering, reflections or glare across the water surface.

Specifying specialist installations may help to reduce maintenance, which can be costly, inconvenient, and involve loss of use of the facility, given the time taken to empty, clear and refill the pool.

Water and air temperatures and ventilation

The hydrotherapy pool and environment should be maintained to ensure maximum comfort and protection of all users[25].

A mechanical supply-and-extract ventilation system should maintain satisfactory internal environmental conditions.

Ventilation should be capable of removing contaminants from the atmosphere within the pool hall and of controlling the air quality, temperature and humidity to ensure user comfort. To achieve these objectives, warm air has to be distributed evenly throughout the enclosure at flow rates that are within acceptable limits for bather comfort.

Recirculation of pool air can be precluded on health grounds – potential build up of the products of disinfection is a suspected cause of respiratory irritation.

Provision and siting of an alarm system should be considered so that staff can summon assistance if required.

Dehumidification is usually needed to prevent condensation on the building structure, and a slightly negative pressure in the pool hall will help to stop moisture permeating the building structure.

Heat reclaim from the exhaust air using heat pumps, heat pipes and/or cross-flow heat exchangers to save energy can halve the energy running costs of a typical pool. Pool covers should be used when a pool is not in use to reduce heat losses and limit the humidity of the air. Consideration should be given to the management/operation of pool covers, and space requirements for their storage.

Water treatment [26]

- The turnover period will vary with the number and type of users and frequency of use.

- The method of water purification needs particular consideration, not only because certain physical problems require that it be especially efficient, but also because some skin conditions may be aggravated by certain chemicals.

- There will need to be automatic rather than manual administration of the necessary chemicals, and the requirements of the Environmental Health Officer will need to be met.

Chemical storage

- Storage facilities should allow chemicals to be stored separately and managed safely in line with current regulations and guidance[27]. Key points include:

- keeping incompatible chemicals apart

- containing chemicals within a bund and separating disinfectant and acid by a bund wall

- keeping chemicals off the floor, with liquids always stored at a low level and no chemicals stored above head height

25. Refer to:
Service Standards of Physiotherapy Practice CSP (2005)
and
Guidance on Good Practice in Hydrotherapy, Hydrotherapy Association of Chartered Physiotherapists – http://www.csp.org.uk/uploads/documents/csp

Management of Spa Pools HPA – http://www.hpa.org.uk/publications/2006/spa_pools/default.htm

26. For advice on water treatment and microbiological health risks, refer to Hygiene for Hydrotherapy Pools, ISBN: 0 901144 460, Public Health Laboratory Service, 1999.

Swimming Pool Water – Pool Water Treatment Advisory Group – http://www.pwtag.org/

27. Refer to:
COSHH
http://www.hse.gov.uk/coshh/

D

28. Refer to:
Fire Safety Risk
Assessment –
Educational Premises –
http://www.communities.
gov.uk/firesafetyguides

BS 5588-8: Fire
precautions in the
design, construction and
use of buildings. Code
of practice for means
of escape for disabled
people –
http://www.bsi-global.
com/shop

BS 8300: The Design
of buildings and their
approaches to meet the
needs of disabled people

Building Bulletin 100
Design for Fire Safety in
Schools, section 4.5.6 –
http://www.teachernet.
gov.uk/sbdupublications/

11d Fire safety and evacuation [28]

All schools have to comply with the Regulatory Reform (Fire Safety) Order 2005 (RRO). The RRO requires a fire safety management plan to be produced as part of the building handover documents. This may require the input of the fire engineer, the school and the fire and rescue service to decide the method of evacuation that is most suitable for the building and its occupants.

Full evacuation lifts should have a separate secure electrical supply and are recommended for means of escape in multi-level special schools.

For some special schools, lifts with very wide doors and very large lift car sizes may be needed to ensure all children can be evacuated quickly and safely. Lifts that are used as a means of escape should be fire resistant and have a separate electrical supply. Guidance on design and use of evacuation lifts is given in BS 5588-8:1999.

Fire alarm and detection systems[29]

The most suitable warning methods will depend on school building occupants. People with visual and hearing impairments, for instance, need a choice of visual, audible systems, or voice announcement systems. Suitable additional visual alarms should be provided in areas where a person may be alone, such as toilets.

There are three types of fire alarm system described in BS 5839:

M – Manual alarm systems

L – Life protection systems

P – Property protection systems

29. Refer to:
BS 5839-1:2002+
A2:2008 Fire detection
and fire alarm systems
for buildings. Code of
practice for system design,
installation, commission-
ing and maintenance.
Clause 18 provides
detailed guidance on the
design and selection of
fire alarm warnings for
people with impaired
hearing (although the
standard is not aimed at
children's settings and
does not cover residential
situations, for which
the requirements are
set out within Approved
Document B) –
http://www.bsi-global.
com/shop

Decisions will need to be taken about whether:

• a life safety (L) and/or property protection (P) system is needed (taking into account the personal educational value of pupils' work)

• a manual or automatic system is suitable

• hold open devices are used

• links are required to a central monitoring station

Whilst a category M system might satisfy Building Regulations, a category L alarm system might better suit a special school, allowing full integration with smoke control and fire extinguishing systems.

Categories of manual call points:

• Type A – direct operation (one action sets off the alarm)

• Type B – indirect operation (two actions set off the alarm – double knock), which may be suitable where tamper-proof installations are required.

Where there are diverse needs, alternative alarm systems may be used:

• Voice alarm system (as part of a public address system)

• Visual (fixed beacons) alarms in certain areas

• Vibrating paging systems for hearing impaired and other disabled people

Fire evacuation

Where a disabled person cannot make their own way out of the building it is the responsibility of management to ensure their safe escape - and personal emergency egress plans (PEEPs) will need to be developed in consultation with them. Escape plans should be posted throughout the building.

The following points need to be considered:

• The means of escape may need more illumination than Illuminated exit signs. Good signage or colour coding of escape routes will be helpful for some people.

• Some people with SEN and disabilities may be confused or have longer reaction times, so travel distances and door widths may be different from those in mainstream schools – escape routes should be wide enough for two wheelchairs side by side.

• Normal circulation routes should be used as emergency evacuation routes and should be accessible at all times.

• Staff communication systems linked with the fire alarm panel will be useful during evacuation.

• The effect of smoke may adversely affect children with complex health needs (such as heart conditions or asthma).

• Staff may need help to open doors during fire evacuation.

• Horizontal evacuation routes reduce the need for evacuation by lift or evacuation chair. Spaces where large numbers gather, such as the school hall, are best located at ground level.

• In vertical evacuation routes, where refuges are provided as a resting or meeting place, they should have a two-way communication system and possibly a video link.

• Where people are descending down stairs at different speeds, a two lane escape can help to prevent accidents from pushing and are easier for evacuation chairs. Stairs may need a minimum width of 1.6m.

• Evacuation lifts with fire protection, operated by management in an emergency, are strongly recommended where there are many children and/or adults with SEN or disabilities.

• Ordinary passenger lifts may be used for evacuation, subject to a risk assessment, if they are located in a fire protected zone, their operation can be ensured during a fire, and robust management procedures can be implemented.

Sprinkler systems

A fire risk assessment must be carried out for all school building projects. The effects of smoke, safety of the occupants and other aspects should be considered along with, for major projects, the use of sprinkler systems and other fire engineering solutions. Schools with significant numbers of children with SEN will generally be considered as medium to high risk[30].

30. Refer to:
Building Bulletin 100 Design for Fire Safety in Schools – http://www.teachernet. gov.uk/sbdupublications/

D

11e Furniture, fittings and equipment (FF&E)

Providing appropriate furniture, fittings and equipment helps to ensure full access to teaching, learning and social activities, regardless of children's disability or SEN.

The brief should outline the FF&E needed for each space in relation to its function, spatial needs and ergonomic design. Advice on specification should be obtained from the LA, school staff, local health services, occupational or physiotherapists and specialist suppliers. The likely use of wheelchairs, mobility equipment and hoists should be established at the briefing stage, as these often require considerable space, both during use and in storage, and can have an impact on the furniture that is compatible.

Once a generic list of FF&E has been determined, layouts should be drawn up. This is a useful way of testing whether spaces are a suitable size and shape. They will provide a basis for discussion when FF&E schedules are finalised with school staff. (See Room layouts, below.) The positions of furniture and equipment should be co-ordinated with the services and structural elements - the position of radiators, for example, dado conduit, electrical switches and data outlets, window sills, shelving and wall fixtures.

Key design issues

The following principles apply to all items:

• FF&E can increase the flexibility of a space. Furniture that is easy to move around or that can be used for more than one purpose can allow for a variety of activities and layouts.

• Furniture must be specified with the needs of the user in mind. Any specialist equipment needs a health and safety risk assessment, which considers the children's SEN or disability. Special enclosures for some equipment may need to be incorporated. Surfaces should be smooth and there should be no sharp edges or projections that could cause harm either by accident or inappropriate use.

• FF&E should be easy to clean and maintain for infection control, avoiding open joints or projections which allow dirt and dust to gather.

• FF&E should be safe, of good quality, fit for purpose and compliant with all relevant British Standards and European Norms. They should be of appropriate fire resistance and 'spread of flame' performance and compliant with health and safety standards.

Furniture standards

The Furniture Industry Research Association (FIRA) offers Certification for School Furniture. Manufacturers must meet requirements in a number of areas such as ergonomics, structural strength, stability and durability, fabric performance, flammability and finishes. Certification provides assurance to schools of fitness for purpose.

The durability and robustness of general school furniture is covered by EN1729, the European Standard for chairs and tables. Purchasing furniture for general classrooms that meets this standard should ensure products are suitable[31].

31. EN1729 will form part of FIRA's certification scheme – www.fira.co.uk

Furniture

Tables and benching

- Work surfaces need to be at a suitable height both for a child's size and for any special needs. (Many electric wheelchairs have a joystick, which adds extra height.) It may be useful to provide various heights of work table (or adjustable height tables but this may be more expensive). Discussions with staff will help specification.

- Forward sloping tables may be appropriate, as there is evidence to suggest they support posture when children are handwriting, improving comfort and concentration. Sloping tables work best with a forward sloping chair.

- Adjustable height units may be operated manually, electrically or electronically. Some schools may need a variety of types to suit children's different needs. All controls must be within reach and easily adjustable for safe, smooth operation and have suitable built-in safety devices, guards or protective facilities. Height adjustable furniture can be heavy and awkward to move, so units on castors may be required to ensure flexibility.

- Particular shapes of worktop may be appropriate, for example work surfaces that 'wrap' around the pupil to provide support for arms. Similarly, tables or chairs that incorporate foot rests can be useful. However, circular tables are unsuitable for wheelchair users, as they prevent pupils getting sufficiently close to the work surface, and tables with modesty panels often prevent wheelchairs getting under the table.

- Work surfaces need to be wide and deep enough to accommodate the necessary learning and communication aids, with objects or fittings in easy reach of the child. There should also be room for an assistant to sit next to the child[32].

- Work surfaces for computers should be deep enough for the keyboard (which may be larger than standard) to be positioned in front of the monitor, and wide enough to accommodate switch access technology either side of the keyboard and monitor. It is particularly important for children with SEN and disabilities to be correctly positioned when they are using a computer - specialist advice from OTs may be needed.

- In practical spaces, work surfaces should be smooth, non-porous, water-resistant and easily cleaned.

- Appropriate colour, without pattern but which provides visual contrast to the surroundings, is useful. FF&E can also provide colour coding or tactile stimuli, if needed.

- Surfaces can contribute to a good acoustic environment. Acoustically reflective materials should be avoided.

- Shiny surfaces reflect light and can reduce visibility.

- Practical spaces need at least one height adjustable sink, along with any adjustable height equipment required for the specialist subject. The mode of

32. Refer to: www.fira.co.uk

operation needs to be safe, easy and suitable for all users.

- There should be enough workspace either side of any sinks for people with SEN and disabilities to work in comfort and safety nearby and there should be accessible fittings, such as lever taps.

- Some tables or benches containing services and power may need to be adjustable to ensure all pupils have full access to all aspects of the curriculum, including food technology, design and technology and science. The extent of this requirement will need to be discussed at an early stage to ensure current and future needs are met.

Chairs

- One-piece moulded chairs are recommended if children are likely to rock backwards and forwards, since they have no fixings that could come loose and cause the seat shell to become detached.

- Where children are prone to incontinence, a polypropylene seat would be appropriate. Some vinyl seat pads feel like fabric.

- A range of chairs of appropriate size with full back support will be needed. Foot rests may also be required. The need for fixed or adjustable height chairs with castors can be assessed but safety and stability should be maintained.

- Forward sloping chairs may be used with the corresponding sloping top table.

- Arms on chairs may provide additional postural support for some pupils.

Storage furniture

- The many two- or three-dimensional objects used as teaching resources and learning aids (especially for children with a visual impairment) can be housed in fixed or adjustable height shelving, low level drawer or cupboard units, trolleys under furniture or full-height cupboards.

- Units that allow people to see their contents are preferred. Tray storage that can be slotted into units at various heights may allow wheelchair users to access their own resources independently.

Other furniture

- A variety of specialist purpose-made items are available for children with SEN and disabilities, such as plastic-coated foam-filled shapes, foam-cushioned support seats or armchairs, rocking and swinging chairs and feeder seats.

- Stable, robust carrels or screens are useful for dividing learning spaces, particularly for pupils with autistic spectrum disorder. Pin boards can be useful for organising subject display, setting the scene and helping children with SEN to engage in and focus on the subject.

- In staff rooms, work surfaces, counters and sinks should suit a variety of users and include some height adjustable units. Staff with disabilities need accessible workstations, facilities and safe circulation to work alongside others.

- Staff office chairs should be fully adjustable, allowing correct positioning for working with ICT. Foot rests should be available and meet the standards of the Health and Safety at Work Act 1974[33].

33. Refer to: http://www.hse.gov.uk/legislation/hswa.htm

Room layouts

Room layouts need to reflect the needs of the children using the space as well as the activities being carried out. For example, a child may need to be in a particular position in the class to support their needs. Furniture and equipment may have to be re-arranged daily to suit varied groupings, activities and diverse needs.

- Loose furniture gives greater flexibility than fixed. Fixed furniture at the perimeter of a space reduces access to valuable wall space.

- Having minimal but versatile FF&E may appear bare but can enable teachers to use stimuli from teaching materials more effectively.

- Having too much FF&E can result in overcrowding and congestion. There should be enough space for everyone to move easily and safely. The likely number of teaching assistants should be considered alongside class sizes[35].

- Considerable space is required for mobility equipment, both in and out of use.

- Ideally ICT should be made accessible in any part of the space by using floor boxes or cable-managed furniture but there must be no trailing leads.

- The interactive whiteboard or a whiteboard and CCTV should be suitably positioned for the type of SEN or disability. Alternatively, 'tablets' may be used.

There are various ways of providing serviced work surfaces in practical spaces[34]:

- Fixed serviced tables located in the middle of the space may restrict the use of the space and flexibility. Carefully positioned fixed service units with loose modular tables allow for a variety of layouts (a).

- Peninsular units mean the teacher has to move in and out of the bays, making supervision more difficult for some children. However, this arrangement can make efficient use of rectangular rooms (b).

- Perimeter benching means children have to turn around to see the teacher, although teachers can easily observe pupils from all parts of the room (c).

See also Practical spaces, page 84.

34. Building Bulletin 80, Science Accommodation in Secondary Schools provides a useful guide to different ways of arranging practical science spaces – http://www.teachernet. gov.uk/sbdupublications/

35. For guidance on distances between tables where there are several wheelchair users in the class, refer to BS 8300: Design of buildings and their approaches to meet the needs of disabled people – http://www.bsi-global. com/shop

D

b

c

a

Furnishings and fittings

Soft furnishings need careful selection for each situation. They may need to withstand frequent washing, and infection control may be an issue, especially where there are children with multiple disabilities and/or complex health needs.

Curtains and blinds

Curtains can add colour and character to a space, absorb sound and provide black-out or dim-out but they can harbour micro-organisms, and need to be laundered frequently, at high temperatures. Any operating controls should be effective, convenient and resistant to unintentional damage.

Blinds are often required to control sunlight or daylight levels for comfort or better visibility. They may also be needed for privacy or to hide an external view to reduce distraction.

Blinds are available in different types: slatted (venetian), roller (in a dense, light or perforated material), vertical or interstitial (between two panes of glass). The final choice will depend on the particular needs of the children but it is worth considering the following:

• Blinds should be water-resistant in wet areas, easy to clean and not collect dust easily. They should not conflict with window openings or reduce natural ventilation.

• Blinds should be adjustable and easy to control but resistant to deliberate or accidental mis-use - captive cords are advisable. Staff should be trained to use blinds properly.

• Fabric blinds should be dense enough to control light adequately. Some slatted blinds can give sharp contrasts of light and shade or a strobe effect, which can affect some people adversely.

• In south facing rooms metal blinds can absorb heat and act like mini radiant panels.

Mobility needs and equipment

Hoists

Staff may need to move disabled children. Health and safety manual handling regulations require the use of a hoist, which can be either portable/ mobile or ceiling-mounted (moving in one or more directions). A combination is often necessary[36].

Ceiling-mounted hoists (see photo below) should be planned at the outset to ensure that the appropriate structural support (bearing in mind that some children may be of adult size), tracking and ceiling heights are provided. Hoist tracking generally requires a ceiling height of about 2.6–2.8m but this should be checked with hoist manufacturers. Tracking should not foul other installations, such as cubicles or curtains. Tracking should not be used to transport a person for a long distance.

Portable hoists (see photo opposite) provide flexibility but require more floor space than ceiling-mounted hoists and

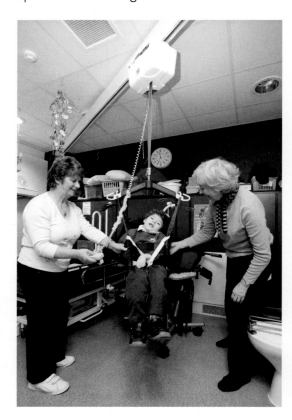

36. Refer to: Health and Safety Matters for Special Educational Needs: Moving and handling – http://www.hse.gov.uk /pubns/

need a space to be stored when not in use. An area of about 1.5–2.5m x 2.5–3.5m is generally needed but dimensions (including turning circle and height) must be checked with manufacturers.

Mobility equipment

Because of the great amount of space required, both in use and for storage, designers need to know about the type and range of mobility equipment and its likely use. It may be useful to consult staff and users.

Disabled children often have three or more pieces of equipment each and use specially fitted wheelchairs to suit their needs. Some disabled children can move unassisted and independently using a combination of indoor and outdoor wheelchairs, walking frames, aids or sticks. They may want to change between different chairs and access mobility storage bays and battery charging equipment without disruption.

Different kinds of mobility equipment are described below:

Small supports, sticks or frames, or mobile walkers – young children may need a clear width of 600/750mm–850/900mm to use sticks, crutches or frames. Children of early years or primary age may use baby walkers or mobility equipment.

Various classroom chairs with padding and support – these can be bulky. Some chairs or trolleys have stands with bases 850–900mm wide, including rubberised tyres on swivel castors.

Large standing frames or side-lying frames – these are large wooden or aluminium framed structures for whole-body support, and a large space is required for their use and storage.

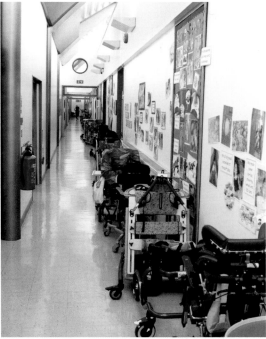

The use and storage of mobility equipment needs to be considered at an early stage to avoid reducing the available circulation space.

D

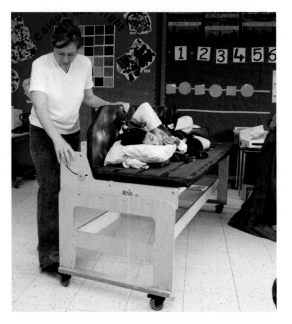

Some children use side-lying frames which take up a lot of space.

37.Refer to:
Manual Handling
Operations Regulations
1992 (as amended)
– Guidance on
Regulations –
http://www.hsebooks.
com/Books/

Wheelchairs

There are three main types of wheelchair.

Self-propelled for independent users with upper body strength. A child may use a self-propelled wheelchair to delay the need for an electric wheelchair.

Electrically propelled four-wheel drive wheelchairs, for independent use controlled by a joystick or other device for indoor and outdoor use, have become wider in recent years. Some children may have less upper body mobility and may not be able to self-propel their wheelchairs, but may be able to manipulate controls to an electrically powered automatic wheelchair. Battery charging facilities and suitable storage are required.

Attendant propelled or assisted-use wheelchairs with small rear wheels and pushed by a carer or support worker are narrower and longer than traditional wheelchairs. Sufficient space should be provided for correct manual handling operations[37].

Wheelchairs may be adapted for the individual (with, for example, foot rests, leg extensions, head rests) and may recline. All this can add to the overall size. The size might also be increased by attachments such as bags for belongings, oxygen packs, large trays for use as a work surface, or speech-communicator devices. BS 8300 can be used as a guide to wheelchair widths and turning circles when assessing spatial requirements but it is important to note that wheelchair sizes change over time and that BS 8300 relates mainly to adults.

Attractive wheelchair design is important for the self esteem of disabled children or young people.

Children often carry their bags on their wheelchairs, which can increase the overall size.

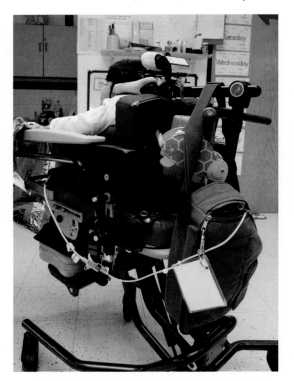

11f Information and communication systems

Information and communication systems are used throught a school for management, safety and security systems as well as teaching and learning.

Networking (wired or wireless) should be available throughout the school, providing flexibility and adaptability but with safe access, avoiding trailing leads, for example.

ICT for infrastructure and management

School staff use ICT for internal communications, management and administration, monitoring progress, and preparing and targeting differentiated learning resources.

The following may need to be provided:

- Intercom, assistance alarms and access control systems
- Panic alarms and/or staff-call systems, subject to risk assessment, where staff need to call for rapid assistance. Simple push-button, pull-cords or radio-tracked alarms worn by staff can be provided in a range of spaces. Loud audible alarms should be avoided where they could cause disruption.

ICT as a learning tool

As well as being a specialist subject in its own right, ICT is a very important tool, which supports and facilitates learning and teaching.

There may also be community use of ICT resources, so facilities such as induction loops, Braille keyboards and so forth may be needed for visitors with disabilities as well as for children and staff.

Whilst everyone should have access to ICT, an appropriate infrastructure should be provided to ensure privacy and security of data and records[38].

Children's equipment needs

In order for children with SEN and disabilities to gain maximum benefit from ICT, their individual sensory and physical needs and abilities have to be understood and appropriate technology provided. For example, a child with a visual impairment may struggle with a whiteboard presentation, but could perhaps use a personal device at their desk to show the content.

A range of ICT equipment is used throughout a school. There is usually one or more networked computer workstation(s) fitted with appropriate access technologies in each teaching space, including a computer workstation or laptop docking station for the teacher. Usually, there are also interactive whiteboards or other interactive teaching technologies and/or plasma screens. Children are increasingly likely to have portable personal technologies such as laptops and other portable battery-operated writing and speech output devices. They might also have one or more specialist devices to help them access ICT, including:

- a larger or alternative mouse (such as switches or a joystick)

38. Refer to: Becta for more on hardware and software for inclusion – http://schools.becta.org.uk/

D

- specialist, including Braille, keyboards
- touch screens (which can help to develop visual skills and hand—eye coordination)
- audio-visual equipment, such as Picture Exchange Communication System (PECS) for children with autistic spectrum disorders
- electronic voice-output communication aids (VOCA) (to support communication difficulty), which will need battery maintenance. They may require, for example, a quiet space, noise-reduction measures, or volume-controlled speakers
- screen magnifiers (for those with a visual impairment), screen readers, and large pointers or contrast settings
- digitised or synthesised sound, which can be used with symbols and pictures for communication tools

- speech reinforcement systems and sound systems — specialist advice will be needed from an acoustic consultant and a relevant therapist. People with hearing impairments can have their needs met by personal aids and room-based equipment.

Other equipment may include:

- mains controller boxes, which are used to enable switches to operate mains powered devices safely, for example switch-operated toys, a food mixer in a cooking session or a radio or television so children can choose when they want to switch it on
- hearing induction loops, radio aids, or sound-field systems (for children with hearing impairment).
- symbol-based learning and communication systems reflecting the symbol and signing taught in the school
- supportive writing software, such as on-screen grids and predictive text, to aid language development

Light, sound and music interaction used in the sensory room or music studio, with networked ICT, supports access to sensory information and social interaction.

A school's current and future ICT vision must be properly understood and integrated into the school design, allowing for flexibility and a mixture of technologies. ICT specialists in using assistive technologies should be consulted at the outset.

Children may use a range of specialist equipment.

Room layouts and furniture

The classroom layout should meet the needs of those likely to use the space. For example, a U-shaped layout with a whiteboard may be suitable for children with hearing impairment.

A whiteboard or plasma screen should be positioned so that everyone can have a clear view and (where relevant) touch the screen.

The following need to be considered to ensure comfortable working positions. (Consultation with the ICT specialist and occupational therapist may be required.)

- The type of table and seat (for example height adjustable)

- The ability to see the computer screen clearly, without glare or shadowing

- Sufficient space to be able to use access devices (such as flat-panel screens, with the computing device located under the desk or to the side, which allows more space for access switches and keyboards)

- Sufficient space for wheelchair users, who may have ICT resources mounted on a tray attached to the wheelchair, on height adjustable tables – alternatively they may use trolleys equipped with a workstation and access devices

- Individual study areas or carrels (which must be large enough for keyboards and other devices) may be used to reduce distraction - useful when speech recognition software is being used, for example, or as docking areas for laptops, enabling access to larger screens

Ceiling-mounted projectors need to be sited for easy maintenance and to avoid damage by children who are active or boisterous.

Hardware

Choosing computers with better energy efficiency will lower heat emissions and reduce the need for additional ventilation and cooling, as well as helping to meet sustainability criteria.

There should be facilities for recharging batteries and equipment as well as secure storage and a technician's workshop/store. Allowance must also be made for a secure server room.

Case studies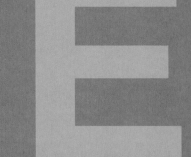

The following case studies illustrate many of the points raised in other sections of this book and show some of the wide range of approaches to meeting the needs of children with SEN and disabilities.

Case study 1: Hollywater School

Client: Hampshire County Council

Architects: P, B & R Design Services

Type: Community special school for pupils with complex learning difficulties

Age range: 2–19

Number on roll: 120

Staff: 80 (60 full-time equivalent)

Date completed: 2006

Area: 3000m²

Cost: £6.3m excluding fees

Context: Two special schools were amalgamated

The site

The new buildings were positioned to make the greatest use of the site, and form a close relationship with the landscape. The general teaching classrooms at the southern edge have views over farmland, shaded by mature oak trees. The mature boundary landscaping and the new building enclose an external play area divided into hard surfaced and grassed play areas, with a fully accessible adventure playground and sensory gardens.

Building design

The building is divided into two main blocks, linked by the learning resource area. The main entrance block contains the community accessible part of the school, with a hydrotherapy pool and main hall and therapy rooms, including soft play and multi-sensory rooms.

The other block houses the teaching spaces, where modules of four classrooms are grouped around a top-lit space, supported by shared small rooms and toilet and changing facilities.

The design gives a sense of progression from early years and primary at one end through secondary to a significantly different and separate post–16 base at the other. There are dedicated support bases for children with PMLD in both primary and secondary.

Colours, carefully chosen to create a calming atmosphere, are used to distinguish different facilities and age groups: warmer, softer colours for reception and infant age children, cooler and more restrained colours for secondary and post 16.

The school library, looking towards the main entrance.

Hollywater School - Floor plan

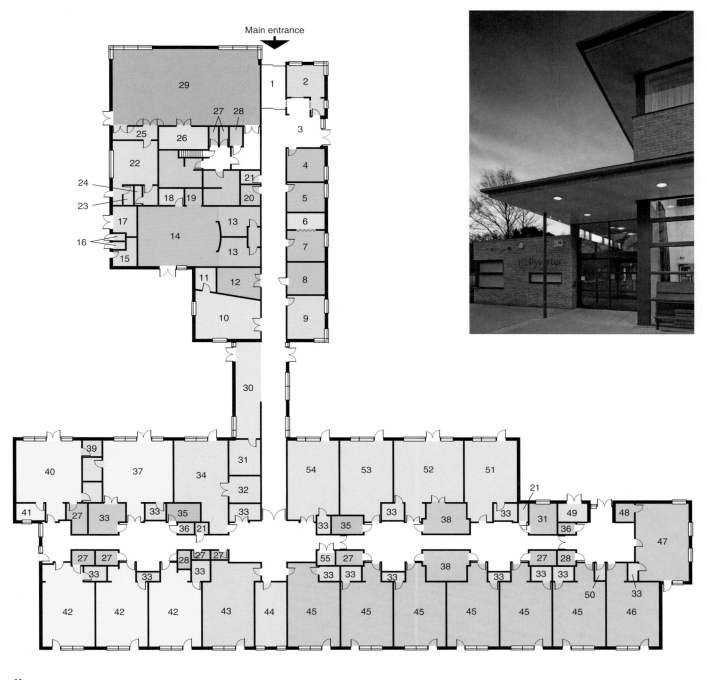

Main entrance

Key:

1	Main entrance lobby
2	Reception/admin
3	Waiting
4	Family/therapists
5	Medical
6	Store
7	Therapists
8	A/V room
9	Head
10	Music
11	Music store
12	Soft play
13	Pool changing
14	Hydrotherapy pool
15	Caretaker
16	Pool chemical store
17	Pool plant
18	Pool store/changing
19	Shower
20	Staff changing
21	Cleaner
22	Kitchen
23	Food store
24	Kitchen toilet
25	Servery/store
26	Hall store
27	Toilet
28	Accessible toilet
29	Hall/dining
30	Library
31	Small group room
32	Art store
33	Store
34	Art
35	Calm room
36	Services/plant
37	Primary PMLD base
38	Hygiene
39	Kitchenette
40	Reception class
41	Quiet room
42	Class base (primary)
43	Staff room
44	ICT resource
45	General teaching (secondary)
46	Leavers' base
47	Life skills
48	Bathroom
49	External store
50	Laundry
51	Design and technology
52	Secondary PMLD base
53	Science
54	Food technology
55	IT server

Colour key:

- Primary
- Secondary
- Specialist teaching/resource
- Admin/staff
- Toilets/changing
- Storage/prep
- Ancillary/plant/clnr/kitchen
- Dining/hall
- Medical/therapy/other support

Access and circulation

There is a long drop-off zone for buses and taxis, with a canopy sheltering the entrance. Automatic sliding doors lead via a lobby to a welcoming reception which overlooks the approach. (See diagram on page 38.)

Circulation spaces are well proportioned and routes simple: the building forms a 'T' shape and there are no interrupting fire doors. (The fire safety strategy includes the use of sprinklers, fire shutters and strategically sited fire doors held open on electromagnetic catches).

Environmental design

A sustainable approach was adopted to maximise natural lighting and ventilation, energy efficiency and links to an attractive landscape. High insulation levels and an airtight building, coupled with surfaces that radiate warmth, help to enhance the quality of life for children who are less active.

The walls and floors of the building are traditional heavy-weight construction, using blocks containing recycled aggregate to provide a high thermal mass for temperature consistency. All classroom roofs are insulated using recycled newspaper, light fittings are low energy, and acoustic measures further enhance the learning environment.

Teaching spaces have:
- balanced and controllable natural light and ventilation
- thermal comfort and good acoustics
- low energy and low glare light fittings (to reduce direct glare to sensitive eyes)
- integral sound-field systems
- interactive whiteboards

The reception area

The secondary art room is a colourful well-lit space.

Case Study 2: Heritage Park Community School

Client: Sheffield City Council

Architects: Sheffield Design and Project Management

Contractor: Wates

Type: Community special school for pupils with behavioural, emotional and social difficulties

Age range: 7–16

Number on roll: 83

Staff: 40

Date completed: September 2005

Area: 2320 m²

Cost: £4.15m

Context: Built as part of a local authority reorganisation of three special schools for BESD to two new schools

The site

The school is on the lower part of a sloping site, set in attractive landscaping. The split level building exploits the site: there is an entrance level car park, zoned play areas for each age group, a hard court for team games and an upper level grass pitch. Perimeter fencing and CCTV cameras provide security.

Building design

Architects worked closely with school staff to produce a building that feels domestic rather than institutional, with a positive ambience that supports wellbeing. Internally the environment is warm and colourful with high quality, robust finishes that withstand wear and look good. Teaching spaces are designed for groups of six to eight children.

The building has three separate suites for Key Stages 2, 3 and 4, each with its own entrance, classrooms, resource areas and small rooms for quiet time or one-to-one work with staff. The youngest primary age children are on the ground floor, with their own library and food room. The older pupils are based on the first floor where they also have access to practical spaces for science, art, design and technology and food technology. A lift and stairs give access to both floors.

Common spaces of a small hall for PE, a dining/meeting room and music space are used on a timetabled basis. These spaces are grouped together near the visitors' entrance, for easy access and to support opportunities for

Heritage Park Community School - Ground and first floor plans

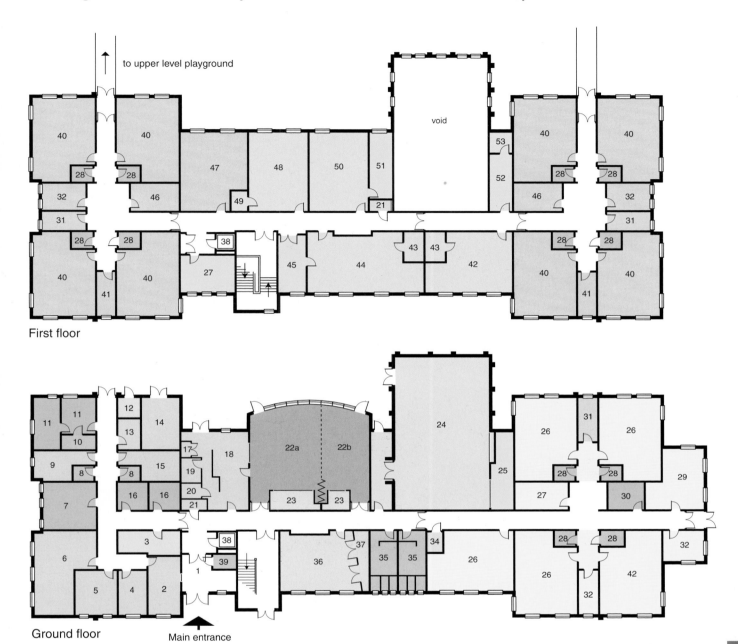

First floor

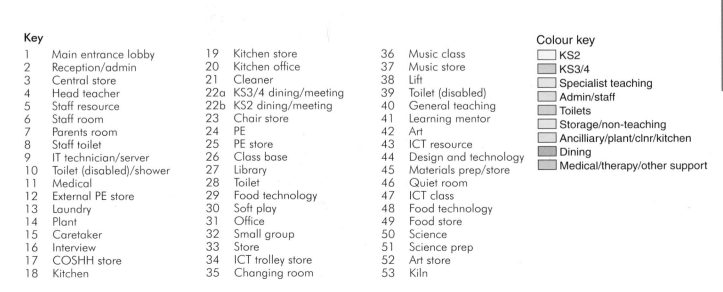

Ground floor

Main entrance

to upper level playground

void

Key

1	Main entrance lobby	19	Kitchen store	36	Music class
2	Reception/admin	20	Kitchen office	37	Music store
3	Central store	21	Cleaner	38	Lift
4	Head teacher	22a	KS3/4 dining/meeting	39	Toilet (disabled)
5	Staff resource	22b	KS2 dining/meeting	40	General teaching
6	Staff room	23	Chair store	41	Learning mentor
7	Parents room	24	PE	42	Art
8	Staff toilet	25	PE store	43	ICT resource
9	IT technician/server	26	Class base	44	Design and technology
10	Toilet (disabled)/shower	27	Library	45	Materials prep/store
11	Medical	28	Toilet	46	Quiet room
12	External PE store	29	Food technology	47	ICT class
13	Laundry	30	Soft play	48	Food technology
14	Plant	31	Office	49	Food store
15	Caretaker	32	Small group	50	Science
16	Interview	33	Store	51	Science prep
17	COSHH store	34	ICT trolley store	52	Art store
18	Kitchen	35	Changing room	53	Kiln

Colour key

- KS2
- KS3/4
- Specialist teaching
- Admin/staff
- Toilets
- Storage/non-teaching
- Ancilliary/plant/clnr/kitchen
- Dining
- Medical/therapy/other support

E

extended school and community use. There is a breakfast club and the main kitchen produces meals on site for the pupils and staff. Also near the main entrance are small spaces for children to work with school and visiting staff and a room for parents to meet and talk with staff.

Teaching spaces provide a comfortable work environment with:

- good room acoustics and sound insulation to aid concentration
- good quality low-glare lighting
- underfloor heating to free up wall space

The school is zoned by age, with suites of secondary classrooms (above) and primary class bases (below).

The food technology room is one of the specialist secondary spaces on the first floor.

Seating alcoves in circulation areas provide a place for informal one-to-one support.

E

Case Study 3: Baytree Community Special School

Client: North Somerset Council

Architects: David Morley Architects

Type: Community special school for children and young people with severe learning disabilities (SLD) and profound and multiple learning difficulties (PMLD)

Age range: 3–19

Number on roll: 67

Date completed: 2004

Cost: £9.2m (for the whole Campus project)

Context: Built as an integrated part of The Campus, incorporating Herons Moor Primary School and community facilities including a library, Council one-stop-shop and adult education rooms.

Site plan

The external space is designed to allow easy access by the children as well as the community. The building has two main entrances – one for the community facilities and one for school use. The roof over-sails a long entrance wall to give a sheltered drop-off for the eight specially equipped mini-buses that bring the special school's students.

Outside there are multi-use games areas, a skate park, bike track, nature garden, adventure area and playing fields.

Building design

North Somerset Council had a vision that 'a school should be a community building that just happens to be used for education'. This inspired both the brief and the building design. The Campus facilities are designed to maximise shared use by the school children and the wider community. Shared areas form the link between the special school and the primary school and between the schools and the community facilities in a way that allows the school and community facilities to expand and contract according to the time of day/week.

The building is conceived as three related wings of accommodation. A top-lit open plan dining hall lies at the heart of the building and can be shared by both the schools and the community, with careful timetabling to ensure the schools have priority. This flexible space has moveable walls so that it can be used not just for dining and assembly but also as a foyer to the main hall for large gatherings or after-school events. The halls and the hydrotherapy pool are positioned for easy access for others visiting the school. The different areas of the school are zoned in a way that retains security and privacy for school pupils.

The special school facilities also include a soft play room and sound and light therapy areas. Each pair of special school class bases shares a small group room and a hygiene room.

Environmental design

The design is focused on natural light and ventilation, making the environment conducive to learning. The two-storey high roof envelope is engineered to allow north light and fresh air to penetrate the spaces below, with reflective shafts allowing light penetration to the back of the lower level classrooms. All classroom windows face south, with projecting canopies and louvres that help control summer sun and allow some free heat from the low winter sun.

Baytree Community Special School - Ground and first floor plans

Key – first floor
1. Primary school class base (KS2)
2. Store
3. Toilets
4. Special school class base
5. Calming room
6. Hygiene
7. Life skills
8. ICT room
9. Art and design
10. Office/admin
11. Staff room
12. Meeting room
13. Adult education
14. Community rooms
15. Plant
16. Void

Key – ground floor
1. Primary school class base (foundation stage)
2. Primary school class base (KS1)
3. Store
4. Medical room
5. Toilets
6. Shower and changing
7. Music
8. Special school class base
9. Calming room
10. Hygiene and changing
11. SEN resource base (PMLD)
12. Multi-purpose room
13. Language and special needs
14. Food technology
15. Speech therapy
16. Schools' reception
17. Soft play
18. Hydrotherapy pool
19. Kitchen
20. Servery
21. Dining
22. Hall
23. Meeting
24. Police office
25. Interview
26. Library and resource centre
27. Library and community reception

Key colours
- Community facilities
- Shared school and community
- Shared support
- Primary school
- Special school

First floor

Ground floor

E

Annexes

F

Annex A:

Legal framework

The Children Act 2004 reformed local authority children's services, bringing together strategic responsibility for education and children's social care under a single Director of Children's Services, along with the requirement for a designated lead member for Children's Services at a political level.

The legislation requires LAs to promote co-operation with each of their local partners (including the police, health, youth justice bodies and others) to ensure that all those delivering children's services and helping to improve children's well-being work together to design and deliver integrated services.

The Children Act provides the legal underpinning for children's trusts, a partnership which also draws in the schools and voluntary sector. All local authority areas are required to produce a single, strategic overarching Children and Young People's Plan (other than LAs with excellent or 'four star' ratings, which are exempt). The CYPP should set out the services affecting children and young people, and help support integrated and effective services that secure better outcomes for all.

Education Act 1996 and the SEN Code of Practice 2001

EA 1996 requires local authorities to identify, assess and make provision for children with special educational needs where necessary. The Act provides for all children to be educated in mainstream schools, including children with a statement of special educational needs, unless this would be incompatible with their parents' wishes or the efficient education of other children.

Following a statutory assessment and the issue of a statement (and in certain other tightly prescribed circumstances), a child may be placed in a special school. Parents have a right of appeal against local authority decisions on assessment and placement.

School governing bodies must use their best endeavours to ensure that appropriate provision is made for pupils with special educational needs.

School Standards and Framework Act 1998 devolves power to LAs to make local school provision following local consultation. Patterns of provision are determined locally following a period of consultation and vary widely. Those proposing any new SEN provision or the reorganisation of existing SEN provision must carry out a SEN Improvement Test[1].

The Disability Discrimination Act 1995 (DDA 1995) requires LAs and governing bodies (GBs) of schools not to discriminate against disabled pupils. They must not treat disabled pupils 'less favourably' and they must make 'reasonable adjustments' for disabled pupils.

The Disability Discrimination Act 2005 extended the **DDA 1995** by placing a duty on all public bodies to promote equality of opportunity for all disabled people. In addition, a specific duty applies to some public authorities, including LAs and GBs of schools. The specific duty includes a requirement to prepare, publish and review a disability equality scheme showing how a public authority is meeting its general duty.

1. Refer to:
Planning and Developing SEN Provision
and
The School Organisation (Establishment and Discontinuance of Schools) Regulations 2007 – Schedule 4, paragraph 20
and
The School Organisation (Prescribed Alterations to Maintained Schools) (England) Regulations 2007 – Schedule 3, paragraphs 18,19 and 20; Schedule 5, paragraphs 18,19 and 20.
All the above at – http://www.dcsf.gov.uk/schoolorg/

Education Act 1996

LAs have a duty to secure sufficient schools to provide for primary and secondary education in their areas and in discharging this duty must, in particular, have regard to the need to secure special educational provision for pupils with SEN.

The Education (School Premises) Regulations 1999

Applying to all schools maintained by LAs, these lay down minimum standards for the premises of most schools, including for toilet facilities and playing fields.

The Education (Independent School Standards) (England) Regulations 2003 lays down minimum standards for independent school premises, similar to the 1999 regulations for maintained schools.

F

Annex B:

Education

Under the Education Act 2002, as amended by the Education Act 2006, LAs and GBs have a duty to exercise their functions with a view to securing for their children a balanced and broadly-based curriculum, which must include the National Curriculum and be taught in a suitable learning environment[2].

The National Curriculum allows individual schools considerable flexibility to develop their own curriculum to meet the needs of the majority of their pupils and to introduce new approaches to teaching and learning. But where the full National Curriculum is not the most appropriate route to maximising pupils' learning and achievement, disapplication of the National Curriculum, under the terms of sections 90 to 93 of the Education Act 2002, may be considered.

Disapplication is permitted:

For individual pupils:

• through a statement of special educational need, under section 92 of the Act

• for a temporary period, through regulations under section 93 of the Act

For groups of pupils or the school community:

• to enable curriculum development or experimentation, under section 90 of the Act

All or part of the curriculum may be disapplied, but schools should ensure pupils' access to a broad and balanced curriculum or learning programme, including as much of the national curriculum as possible.

The National Curriculum Inclusion Statement emphasises the importance of providing effective learning opportunities for all children and puts forward three key principles for inclusion:

• Setting suitable learning challenges

• Responding to children's diverse learning needs

• Overcoming potential barriers to learning by using the outcomes of assessments for individuals and/or groups of children.

National Curriculum assessment is carried out through eight levels (levels 1 to 8) and across all the key stages. A few children may be working at early developmental stages of communicating, interacting and learning. P scales are differentiated performance criteria which describe attainment in eight stages for pupils below level 1 of the National Curriculum.

Children with SEN and disabilities achieve across the whole spectrum of attainment and progress in varied ways. At the age of 16, some young people will attain GCSEs and/or vocational qualifications and remain at school or transfer to a further education college. Others may be achieving at the lower National Curriculum levels or on the P scales.

2. A statement of SEN may provide for the disapplication or modification of the National Curriculum for a specific child.

Table 38: The phases of education

Phase	Age	Year	Key stage
Early years	3 – 4	Nursery	
	4 – 5	Reception	
Primary	5 – 7	1 – 2	1
	7–11	3 – 6	2
Secondary	11–14	7 – 9	3
	14–16	10–11	4
Post 16	16–19	12–13	

F

Annex C:

Special school provision

Special schools maintained by the LA comprise community special schools and foundation special schools. Under certain circumstances, LAs may place children in independent or non-maintained special schools.

Non–maintained special schools (NMSS)

These schools are not maintained by LAs and are approved under Section 342 of the Education Act 1996. They are non-profit-making and run by charities or charitable trusts. An LA may place a child in a NMSS following a statutory assessment and the issue of a statement naming that school. NMSS are subject to the provisions set out in the Education (Non-maintained Special Schools) (England) Regulations 1999. These Regulations deal with the initial and continuing conditions for approval by the Secretary of State, which relate to issues of governance, health and safety, premises, and the non-profit-making status of the school.

Independent schools

Many children with SEN attend independent schools. Some independent schools cater wholly or mainly for children with SEN. Independent schools are not required to teach the National Curriculum, although many do[3]. The Education (Independent School Standards) (England) Regulations 2003 set out the statutory requirements for independent school premises, the full-time educational provision and a broad curriculum appropriate for the ages and aptitudes of children. They also provide that where schools admit children with statements of SEN they must fulfil the requirements of the statement. There should be suitably qualified specialist and support staff and accommodation to support these requirements.

Residential special schools

Some children with SEN attend residential special schools: as an essential part of their educational programme; to stabilise school attendance; and/or to help families resolve social issues or to provide respite. The special school is firstly a school and must comply with all legislation concerning the provision of education that applies to schools.

The National Care Standards 2000 apply to the residential/care accommodation at residential special schools. Ofsted has responsibility for welfare inspection of the residential accommodation of boarding schools, including residential special schools.

Residential special schools are distinct from respite accommodation, other boarding schools and children's homes. However, boarding schools that accommodate, or make accommodation arrangements for, any child for more than 295 days a year, are required to register as children's homes with Ofsted. Such schools are then subject to the Children's Homes Regulations 2001 and the national minimum standards for children's homes.

3. Where a school admits a child with a statement which provides that they must be taught the National Curriculum or parts of it, the school must make the necessary provision to meet those requirements.

Annex D:

Planning for accessibility

Under the Planning duties in Part 4 of the Disability Discrimination Act (DDA), local authorities are required to develop **accessibility strategies** and schools to develop **accessibility plans,** to improve access to school education for disabled pupils. This includes making any necessary improvements to the physical environment of the school (such as rearranging room space, removing obstructions from walkways) and physical aids to accessing education (such as ramps, widened doorways, adapted toilets, and wayfinding systems).

An **access statement** has to be produced as part of the LA's planning approval process. This is a description of how inclusive design principles have been incorporated into a development. It explains how the building meets or deviates from standard guidance and how an accessible service is to be provided from the building, both now and in the future.

This building bulletin can be used as a reference when assessing accessibility but a full **accessibility audit** should be carried out by building professionals. Other useful guides to assessing accessibility are listed right.

References

Accessible Schools: Summary Guidance
DCSF, 2002, Ref: DfES/0462/2002
Contains guidance for LAs and schools on planning to increase the accessibility of schools to disabled pupils
http://publications.teachernet.gov.uk/

Planning Duties in Part 4 of the Disability Discrimination Act (DDA) – DCSF guidance
http://www.teachernet.gov.uk/wholeschool/disability/disabilityandthedda/

Design and Access Statements: How to write, read and use them
The Commission for Architecture and the Built Environment (CABE) 2006
http://www.cabe.org.uk/publications

Inclusive Projects
Disabled Persons Transport and Advisory Committee, 2003, Best practice advice on how all participants in the development process can contribute to the delivery of a high quality inclusive environment
http://www.dptac.gov.uk/inclusive/guide/index.htm

Planning and Access for Disabled People: A good practice guide
http://www.communities.gov.uk/publications/planningandbuilding/planningaccess

The Building Regulations Approved Document M 2005
http://www.planningportal.gov.uk/buildingregulations

BS 8300: Design of buildings and their approaches to meet the needs of disabled people
http://www.bsi-global.com/shop

Easy Access to Historic Buildings
English Heritage 2004, Product code 50702
http://www.english-heritage.org.uk/publications

The National Register of Access Consultants
A useful list of resources on accessibility
http://www.nrac.org.uk

Exploring Access in Mainstream
How to audit your school environment, focusing on the needs of pupils who have visual impairment ISBN: 1858786304 available from RNIB bookshops
http://onlineshop.rnib.org.uk/

F

Annex E:

Typical model schedules for special schools

Special schools vary according to local approach, the type and range of children's needs (both at the school and in the wider community) and the type of extended school and community services provided. The schedules shown on the following pages, which are consistent with the area guidelines given in the rest of the book, are intended as guidelines, to form a basis from which LAs and schools can build up their own school schedules to suit local needs.

All models take account of a child's full curriculum entitlement and their medical and therapy needs, as well as extended school and community use, multi-agency working, training and outreach. All are based on a class group size of eight.

The figure for circulation of 25 per cent of the gross area takes account of the needs of children who use mobility aids and children who need more space between themselves and others. The partitions' allowance of 4 per cent of gross area reflects the fact that special schools have a number of small rooms and often thicker partitions for acoustic reasons.

Three school types are shown (A, B and D, taken from the four types A, B, C and D referred to earlier in the document), reflecting typical ranges of need. The assumptions behind the models are described below. For more information about children's needs, see page 12. At the time of writing, the DCSF is planning to put additional model schedules on the website www.teachernet.gov.uk/schoolbuildings , including for all-age schools.

4. For schools with less than 50 per cent of pupils with profound and multiple learning difficulties or significant physical difficulties (range C), schedules would be similar to those shown for range D but with marginally less area overall.

Range A

Pupils have behaviour, emotional and social difficulties as their main SEN. (Typically there are more boys than girls.) Pupils are mostly ambulant, very active, rarely have physical disabilities but need more personal space for their behaviour needs. There may be outreach programmes with local schools or links with a local pupil referral unit. There is a high need for storage for safety, security and to minimise distractions in class, but items of equipment are less bulky than at other special schools.

Range B

Pupils' needs cover a wide range, including moderate or severe learning difficulties, speech, language and communication needs, and ASD. No children have profound and multiple learning difficulties. Some pupils are ambulant, some are active or have behaviour needs but others may have minor physical disabilities. Some may have severe sensory impairment. Support spaces include sensory rooms, soft play (primary), and therapy bases such as speech and language therapy or sensory support, but no hydrotherapy. A few children use mobility aids.

Range D[4]

Pupils' needs cover a wide range, including moderate or severe learning difficulties, speech, language and communication needs, and severe ASD. More than 50 per cent have profound and multiple learning difficulties. Some pupils are ambulant and active, some may have behaviour needs but others (more than 50 per cent) have significant physical disabilities. Most of the children have sensory impairments and many have multiple disabilities. Support spaces include sensory rooms, soft play (mainly primary), hydrotherapy, physiotherapy and specialist changing rooms. The areas allow for the use and storage of mobility equipment.

All secondary models show post-16 provision as an option, providing tutor bases and common room facilities. The models assume that some pupils will attend an FE college or a work placement, or access community facilities (where suitable support facilities will be needed). If students stay on the school site to follow vocational courses, additional area to that shown here will be needed.

If these model schedules are used to build up a schedule of accommodation for a co-located special school, allowance will need to be made for any shared spaces. The gross area is likely to be less than in the examples shown here.

Below are three early years model schedules. These are assumed to be attached to a primary or all-age school and therefore have their own entrance, office and some support spaces but some sharing of spaces such as the main staff room, hall and therapy spaces is assumed. All models are based on one group of eight children. A two group unit would need an extra play room and additional associated spaces (for example, toilets, store rooms) but core facilities (for example, office, kitchen, soft play area) would be the same.

Example schedules for different types of early years unit

Range		A			B			D		
Number of children (FTE)		8			8			8		
Type of space	Notes	Area (m^2)	No. of rooms	Total area (m^2)	Area (m^2)	No. of rooms	Total area (m^2)	Area (m^2)	No. of rooms	Total area (m^2)
Learning and support	1									
Play space		65	1	65	65	1	65	75	1	75
Small group room		12	1	12	12	1	12	12	1	12
Sensory/soft play					12	1	12	12	1	12
Social skills base	2	20	1	20						0
Parents' room		8	1	8	8	1	8	8	1	8
Staff areas										
Office		9	1	9	9	1	9	9	1	9
Visiting professional/interview/assessment		12	1	12	12	1	12	12	1	12
Storage										
Play room equipment (indoor)		2	1	2	2	1	2	2	1	2
Play room equipment (outdoor)		4	1	4	4	1	4	4	1	4
Mobility equipment/buggy store		3	1	3	5	1	5	10	1	10
Supplies store		2	1	2	2	1	2	2	1	2
Cleaners' store		2	1	2	2	1	2	2	1	2
TOTAL NET AREA				**139**			**133**			**148**
Kitchen		6	1	6	6	1	6	6	1	6
Pupil toilets/change		16	1	16	16	1	16	25	1	25
Staff toilets		3	1	3	3	1	3	3	1	3
Visitor/disabled toilet		4	1	4	4	1	4	4	1	4
Laundry		2	1	2	2	1	2	4	1	4
Circulation			25%	54		25%	52		25%	60
Partitions			4%	10		4%	9		4%	11
TOTAL NON-NET AREA				**95**			**92**			**113**
TOTAL GROSS AREA				**234**			**225**			**261**

1. Could also be used as a basis for a nurture group

2. One area or a few small spaces set up as a dining/sitting/family room

Example schedules for different types and sizes of primary special schools

Range FE Pupil places	Notes	A 1 56 Area (m²)	No. of rooms	Total area (m²)	B 2 112 Area (m²)	No. of rooms	Total area (m²)	D 1.5 88 Area (m²)	No. of rooms	Total area (m²)
Classrooms/bases	1									
Reception		65	1	65	65	2	130	75	2	150
KS1 and KS2		52	6	312	60	12	720	65	9	585
Practical spaces	2									
Art/science/D&T		25	1	25	25	1	25	25	1	25
Food technology		25	1	25	25	1	25	25	1	25
Music/movement/drama	3									
Music drama/large group room					60	1	60	65	1	65
Learning resource spaces										
Small group room	4	10	4	40	10	7	70	12	6	72
Library	5	15	1	15	20	1	20	15	1	15
ICT (class/resource)		15	1	15	20	1	20	15	1	15
SEN resource base	6				30	1	30	30	1	30
Halls & dining	7									
Hall		100	1	100	100	1	100	100	1	100
Dining		80	1	80	125	1	125	110	1	110
Medical, therapy & other support										
Medical/school nurse's room	8	15	1	15	15	1	15	15	2	30
Physiotherapy								30	1	30
Therapy/specialist support	9	15	1	15	15	1	15	15	1	15
Sensory room/studio	10				24	1	24	24	1	24
Hydrotherapy	11							85	1	85
Social skills/'home' base	12	20	2	40						
Soft play					24	1	24	24	1	24
Calming room		10	1	1	10	1	10	10	1	10
Parents' room		15	1	15	15	1	15	15	1	15
Staff areas										
Reception/admin		20	1	20	20	1	20	20	1	20
Head teacher		15	1	15	15	1	15	15	1	15
Deputy		10	1	10	10	1	10	10	1	10
Premises manager		10	1	10	10	1	10	10	1	10
Meeting/training room		20	1	20	25	1	25	20	1	20
Visiting professionals' office		15	1	15	15	1	15	15	1	15
Staff room		40	1	40	60	1	60	50	1	50
Staff preparation room		20	1	20	25	1	25	20	1	20
Storage										
Coats & bags		2	7	14	2	14	28	2	11	22
Mobility equipment (bays)					5	14	70	10	11	110
Classroom resources		4	7	28	4	14	56	4	11	44
Art/science/D&T resources		4	1	4	4	1	4	4	1	4
Food tech resources		3	1	3	3	1	3	3	1	3
Drama/music store		8	1	8	8	1	8	8	1	8
Library store		4	1	4	4	1	4	4	1	4
ICT store		4	1	4	4	1	4	4	1	4
SEN resource base store					4	1	4	4	1	4
PE store		12	1	12	10	1	10	10	1	10
Furniture	13	8	1	8	12	1	12	10	1	10
Extended/community use		8	1	8	8	1	8	8	1	8
Social skills base store		1	2	2						
Medical/communication aids/equipment					5	1	5	5	1	5
Therapy store					4	1	4	4	1	4
Oxygen cylinders								2	1	2
Pool store (chemicals)								6	1	6
Visiting professionals' store		2	1	2	2	1	2	2	1	2
Meeting/training room store		2	1	2	2	1	2	2	1	2
Equipment store					5	1	5	5	1	5
Admin store	14	4	1	4	4	1	4	4	1	4
Central teaching resources		14	1	14	20	1	20	18	1	18

Continued

Type of space	Notes	Range FE Pupil places								
		A 1 56			**B** 2 112			**D** 1.5 88		
		Area (m²)	No. of rooms	Total area (m²)	Area (m²)	No. of rooms	Total area (m²)	Area (m²)	No. of rooms	Total area (m²)
Premises store		9	1	9	9	1	9	9	1	9
Cleaners' store		2	2	4	2	3	6	2	2	4
General stores	15	10	1	10	10	1	10	10	1	10
External store (PE/play equipment)		10	1	10	10	1	10	10	1	10
External store (maintenance)		10	1	10	10	1	10	10	1	10
TOTAL NET AREA				**1082**			**1906**			**1912**
Toilets and changing										
Pupil toilets	16	8	5	40	8	8	64	8	5	40
Pupil hygiene	17	12	1	12	15	2	30	15	5	75
Laundry		6	1	6	6	1	6	6	1	6
Pupil changing - hall	18	14	2	28	16	2	32	16	2	32
Pupil changing - pool	19							30	2	60
Staff toilets		4	4	16	4	6	24	4	4	16
Disabled toilets	20	4	2	8	4	2	8	4	2	8
Staff change and lockers		8	2	16	15	2	30	10	2	20
Staff change - hall		4	2	8	4	2	8	4	2	8
Staff change - pool								4	2	8
Kitchen										
Kitchen		35	1	35	50	1	50	40	1	40
Servery		10	1	10	10	1	10	10	1	10
Kitchen office		6	1	6	6	1	6	6	1	6
Kitchen food store		6	1	6	6	1	6	6	1	6
Kitchen refuse store		6	1	6	6	1	6	6	1	6
Kitchen cleaner		2	1	2	2	1	2	2	1	2
Kitchen toilet/change		4	1	4	4	1	4	4	1	4
Other										
Plant		45	1	45	75	1	75	65	1	65
Pool plant								20	1	20
File server		4	1	4	4	1	4	4	1	4
Circulation % GA	21		25%	470		25%	800		25%	827
Partitions % GA			4%	75		4%	128		4%	132
TOTAL NON-NET AREA				**797**			**1293**			**1395**
TOTAL GROSS AREA				**1879**			**3199**			**3307**

Primary schedule notes

1. Groups up to 8. Direct access to external area ideally, safety and security issues need careful consideration.
2. Could take place in zoned area of classroom if big enough but consider hygiene and safety.
3. Possible use for breakfast/after-school clubs, maybe sliding folding doors to hall. Range A school use dining room for music/drama.
4. One between two classrooms, average size shown.
5. Separate library or combined with ICT resource below.
6. Timetabled for extra support to small groups e.g. children with PMLD or ASD.
7. Sliding folding doors between gives flexibility.
8. Second room as nurse's room needed if high % PMLD.
9. Depends on children's needs, e.g. speech and language base, VI/HI support.
10. One large or two small spaces.
11. 24m² pool with 2–2.5m wide surround.
12. Two small spaces or one large space e.g. to simulate family living room or for nurture group room, can be used in conjunction with food tech.
13. Tables and chairs to clear hall.
14. Stationery and secure records.
15. Bulk items.
16. Ratio of boys to girls to be considered, especially in type A. May need to be larger if community use.
17. Size depends on layout chosen.
18. Ratio of boys to girls to be considered especially in type A. May need to be larger if community use.
19. Including showers, toilets and lockers.
20. Additional toilets may be required to meet Building Regulations ADM, depending on layout.
21. Includes reception area and secure lobby.

F

Example schedules for different types and sizes of secondary special schools

Range		A			B			D		
FE		1.5			2.5			1.5		
Pupil places (11–16)		64			96			64		
Pupil places (post–16)		24			40			24		
Type of space	Notes	Area (m²)	No. of rooms	Total area (m²)	Area (m²)	No. of rooms	Total area (m²)	Area (m²)	No. of rooms	Total area (m²)
General teaching spaces	1									
KS3 and KS4		52	8	416	60	12	720	65	8	520
Practical spaces	2									
Science		65	1	65	60	1	60	65	1	65
Design & technology (inc. CAD/CAM)		75	1	75	65	1	65	70	1	70
Food technology		65	1	65	60	1	60	65	1	65
Art		65	1	65	60	1	60	65	1	65
Music/movement/drama	3									
Music/drama		80	1	80	65	1	65	70	1	70
Learning resource spaces										
Small group room	4	14	4	56	14	6	84	14	4	56
Library	5	55	1	55	40	1	40	30	1	30
ICT (class/resource)		60	1	60	30	1	30	30	1	30
SEN resource base	6				30	2	60	30	2	60
Kiln room		4	1	4	4	1	4	4	1	4
Recording room		15	1	15						
Halls & dining	7									
Hall		306	1	306	140	1	140	140	1	140
Dining		90	1	90	110	1	110	100	1	100
Medical, therapy & other support										
Medical/school nurse's room	8	15	1	15	15	1	15	15	2	30
Physiotherapy								30	1	30
Therapy/specialist support	9	15	1	15	15	2	30	15	2	30
Sensory room/studio	10				24	1	24	24	1	24
Hydrotherapy	11							85	1	85
Social skills base	12	25	2	50						
Social recreation		30	1	30						
Calming room		10	1	10	10	1	10	10	1	10
Parents' room		15	1	15	15	1	15	15	1	15
Staff areas										
Reception/admin		20	1	20	20	1	20	20	1	20
Head teacher		15	1	15	15	1	15	15	1	15
Deputy		10	1	10	10	2	20	10	1	10
Premises manager		10	1	10	10	1	10	10	1	10
Meeting/training room		20	1	20	25	1	25	20	1	20
Visiting professionals' office		15	1	15	15	1	15	15	1	15
Staff room		40	1	40	55	1	55	40	1	40
Staff preparation room		20	1	20	25	1	25	20	1	20
Interview room		12	1	12						
Storage & prep										
Coats & bags	13	2	8	16	2	12	24	2	8	16
Mobility equipment (bays)	14				5	12	60	10	8	80
General teaching resources		4	8	32	4	12	48	6	8	48
Science prep/store		15	1	15	15	1	15	15	1	15
D&T resources		8	1	8	8	1	8	8	1	8
D&T work in progress		7	1	7	7	1	7	7	1	7
Food tech (food)		4	1	4	4	1	4	4	1	4
Food tech (resources)		4	1	4	4	1	4	4	1	4
Art resources		7	1	7	7	1	7	7	1	7
Art work in progress		6	1	6	6	1	6	6	1	6
Drama/music store		10	1	10	10	1	10	10	1	10
Library store		4	1	4	4	1	4	4	1	4
ICT store		4	1	4	4	1	4	4	1	4
SEN resource base store					4	1	4	4	1	4
PE store	15	30	1	30	18	1	18	18	1	18
Furniture	16	12	1	12	18	1	18	12	1	12

Continued

Range FE Pupil places (11–16) Pupil places (post–16)		A 1.5 64 24			B 2.5 96 40			D 1.5 64 24		
Type of space	Notes	Area (m²)	No. of rooms	Total area (m²)	Area (m²)	No. of rooms	Total area (m²)	Area (m²)	No. of rooms	Total area (m²)
Extended/community use		8	1	8	8	1	8	8	1	8
Social skills base store		1	2	2						
Medical/communication aids/equipment					5	1	5	5	1	5
Therapy store								4	1	4
Oxygen cylinders								2	1	2
Pool store (chemicals)								6	1	6
Visiting professionals' store		2	1	2	2	1	2	2	1	2
Meeting/training room store		2	1	2	2	1	2	2	1	2
Equipment store								5	1	5
Admin store	17	4	1	4	4	1	4	4	1	4
Central teaching resources		18	1	18	22	1	22	18	1	18
Premises store	18	9	1	9	9	1	9	9	1	9
Cleaners' store		2	2	4	2	4	8	2	2	4
General stores	19	10	1	10	10	1	10	10	1	10
External store (PE/play equipment)		15	1	15	15	1	15	15	1	15
External store (maintenance)		10	1	10	10	1	10	10	1	10
TOTAL NET AREA				**1892**			**2113**			**2000**
Toilets and changing										
Pupil toilets	20	8	7	56	8	10	80	8	6	48
Pupil hygiene	21	12	1	12	15	3	45	20	5	100
Laundry		6	1	6	6	1	6	6	1	6
Pupil changing - hall	22	20	2	40	16	2	32	16	2	32
Pupil changing (wet) - pool	23							30	2	60
Staff toilets		4	4	16	4	8	32	4	4	16
Disabled toilets	24	4	2	8	4	2	8	4	2	8
Staff change and lockers		10	2	20	20	2	40	10	2	20
Staff change - hall		8	2	16	4	2	8	4	2	8
Staff change - pool								4	2	8
Kitchens										
Kitchen		40	1	40	60	1	60	40	1	40
Servery		10	1	10	10	1	10	10	1	10
Kitchen office		6	1	6	6	1	6	6	1	6
Kitchen food store		6	1	6	6	1	6	6	1	6
Kitchen refuse store		6	1	6	6	1	6	6	1	6
Kitchen cleaner		2	1	2	2	1	2	2	1	2
Kitchen toilet/change		4	1	4	4	1	4	4	1	4
Other										
Plant		75	1	75	85	1	85	80	1	80
Pool plant								20	1	20
File server		4	1	4	4	1	4	4	1	4
Circulation % GA	25		25%	781		25%	897		25%	875
Partitions % GA			4%	125		4%	143		4%	140
TOTAL NON-NET AREA				**1233**			**1474**			**1499**
TOTAL GROSS AREA (11-16)				**3125**			**3587**			**3499**

Table continued on page 196

Post 16

Range		A			B			D		
FE		1.5			2.5			1.5		
Pupil places (11–16)		64			96			64		
Pupil places (post–16)		24			40			24		
Type of space	Notes	Area (m^2)	No. of rooms	Total area (m^2)	Area (m^2)	No. of rooms	Total area (m^2)	Area (m^2)	No. of rooms	Total area (m^2)
Post 16										
Teaching/tutor base		52	3	156	60	5	300	65	3	195
Common room		40	1	40	70	1	70	50	1	50
Extra/over dining		20	1	20	30	1	30	25	1	25
Small group rooms		15	1	15	15	3	45	15	2	30
Extra/over staff room		10	1	10	15	1	15	10	1	10
Extra/over staff preparation room		8	1	8	12	1	12	8	1	8
Mobility equipment (bays)	26				5	5	25	10	3	30
Teaching resources storage		4	3	12	4	5	20	4	3	12
Common room store		4	1	4	4	1	4	4	1	4
TOTAL NET AREA				**265**			**521**			**364**
Toilets/hygiene		8	2	16	20	3	60	20	2	40
Staff toilets		4	2	8	4	2	8	4	2	8
Circulation % GA			25%	102		25%	207		25%	145
Partitions			4%	16		4%	33		4%	23
TOTAL NON-NET AREA				**142**			**308**			**216**
TOTAL GROSS AREA (post-16)				**407**			**829**			**580**
TOTAL GROSS AREA 11-18				**3532**			**4416**			**4079**

Secondary schedule notes

1. Subject/tutor bases for groups up to 8.
2. For whole or half class groups. Type A D&T includes an allowance for CAD/CAM facilities. Safety a particular issue in science and D&T.
3. Musical instruments, especially drum kits, space consuming. May have acoustic sliding folding doors to hall.
4. One between two classrooms (min 2 per key stage), average size shown.
5. Types B & D separate library or combined with ICT resource below. Type A library and separate ICT class/resource space.
6. Timetabled for extra support to small groups, e.g. children with PMLD or ASD.
7. Sliding folding doors between gives flexibility. 306m² gives 2 badminton courts. 140m² could be increased to 180m² for community badminton. Consider extended school use. Halls may be used for music and drama, consider sliding folding doors to music/drama space.
8. Second room as nurse's room (clinics/feed preparation).
9. Depends on children's needs, e.g. speech and language base, VI/HI support.
10. One large or two small spaces.
11. 24m² pool with 2-2.5m wide surround.
12. 1 per key stage for PSHE/careers/social skills.
13. May be in lockers off circulation areas or in classroom (area in addition to classroom).
14. Generally in bays off circulation but may be in enclosed store.
15. Shape of space determined by bulky equipment e.g. trampoline. May need more if community use.
16. Tables and chairs to clear hall.
17. Stationery and secure records.
18. May include SEN technical aids.
19. Bulk items.
20. Ratio of boys to girls to be considered, especially in type A. May need to be larger if community use.
21. Size depends on layout chosen.
22. Ratio of boys to girls to be considered, especially in type A. May need to be larger if community use.
23. Including showers, toilets, lockers.
24. Additional toilets may be required to meet Building Regulations A D M, depending on layout.
25. Includes reception area and secure lobby.
26. See note 14.

F

Annex F:

Designing for children's needs - a checklist

The table below is a guide to some of the key design points associated with specific needs. Each child is unique, however, and may have several of these needs. See page 12 for a broad description of children's needs. Needing space for assistants alongside is common to all.

Children's need	Typical support	Design issues	Space needed in classroom for...
Cognition and learning			
Specific learning difficulty SpLD	3D learning aids; occupational and/or physiotherapy; learning, behaviour/speech & language (SpLg) support	Good acoustics for SpLg therapy; storage for learning aids; SEN resource base	Learning aids, ICT; practical work; flexible layouts for movement work; appropriate positioning of child in class
Moderate learning difficulty MLD	SpLg therapy; learning & behaviour support; social skills training	Good visibility for supervision; good acoustics for SpLg; H&S risk assessments; storage for resources and learning aids; SEN resource & specialist bases	Learning aids, ICT; practical work; flexible use of FF&E; appropriate positioning of child in class
Severe learning difficulty SLD	3D learning aids; multi-sensory work; adapted ICT; social skills & independence training; SpLg therapy; learning & behaviour support; physio-, occupational & hydrotherapy	Good visibility for supervision; wayfinding to aid independence; good acoustics for SpLg therapy; specialist SEN support; H&S risk assessments; storage & use of mobility/learning aids	Multi-sensory and practical activities; learning aids, ICT; flexible use of FF&E; movement and circulation (some mobility aids); additional support staff
Profound & multiple learning difficulty PMLD	3D learning aids; multi-sensory work; sensory impairment support; SpLg therapy; occupational, physio-and/or hydrotherapy; medical & personal care; soft play	As SLD but more space for greater support, storage and concentration of needs; higher accessibility standards; intensive use of mobility aids & hoists; H&S risk assessments: manual handling, infection control; storage and use of mobility & learning aids	Multi-sensory, practical & therapy work; adapted ICT & access technology; additional staff; flexible use of FF&E; movement and circulation (bulky mobility aids)
Behaviour, emotional and social development			
Behaviour, emotional and social difficulty BESD	Behavioural, cognitive, social skills support; learning mentors; social workers, educational psychologists, mental health service (CAMHS)	Good sightlines, balance between privacy and ease of overseeing children; secure storage; robust materials, tamper proof FF&E & concealed services; H&S risk assessments; large spaces for social and outdoor activities	Avoiding distraction and conflict; varying layout (e.g. separated or grouped tables); supervision; developing social skills; quiet/informal corner
Communication and interaction			
Speech, language & communication needs SLCN	Social skills support; learning & communication aids, synthetic speech production equipment, assistive technology; SpLg therapy; learning and behaviour support	Easily understood whole school layout with clear signage; good lighting, room acoustics and sound insulation; sound-field systems, extra ICT and associated services	Position of child in class; use of signs, symbols, communication aids and synthetic speech production equipment; SpLg therapy

Continued

Children's need	Typical support	Design issues	Space needed in classroom for...
Autistic spectrum disorder ASD	Learning & behaviour support; social skills programmes in class and by withdrawal; specialist ASD teaching approaches; specialist ASD resource base	Simple layout: calm, ordered, low stimulus spaces, no confusing large spaces; indirect lighting, no glare, subdued colours; good acoustics, avoiding sudden/background noise; robust materials, tamper-proof elements and concealed services; possibly H&S risk assessments; safe indoor and outdoor places for withdrawal and to calm down	Varying approaches; structured activities using ICT and FF&E; position of child in class; screened workstations; safe quiet place to calm down
Sensory and/or physical			
Hearing impairment HI	Use of CCTV; HI teaching strategies; oral signing; HI learning & communication support; Splg therapy & social skills training; audiology & HI assessment	Avoid distraction: low sensory stimulus & subdued colours; good quality low glare lighting, avoiding shadows & silhouetting; good quality acoustics, low background noise; visual alarms, sound-field systems, hearing loops; storage & maintenance of technical aids	Signing, communication worker; U-shaped or other layout for good visibility; visual aids/ICT/TV/CCTV; radio aids
Visual impairment VI	VI specialist aids e.g. tactile and visual aids, Braille, CCTV viewers, ICT text magnification, speech & sound output; VI teaching strategies; VI support by mobility training officer	Good quality ambient & task lighting & controls; visual contrast, cues, symbols, tactile trails & maps; good acoustics, low background noise, speech & audio aids; sounder alarms, H&S warnings; VI resource room; storage and maintenance of technical aids	Clear, safe uncluttered layout; specialist (e.g. tactile and visual) aids; adapted ICT
Multi-sensory impairment MSI	Visual, tactile, mobility, communication aids and multi-sensory work; varied support as needed; MSI assessment, 1-1 learning and behaviour work; soft play room	As for HI and VI: clear, simple layout for sensory wayfinding with visual, audio & tactile cues; good quality non-glare lighting; good quality room acoustics, no background noise; greater use of mobility aids, hoists & hydrotherapy (see PD); large store	Individual or small groups, with HI, VI, MSI workers; practical learning aids; multi-sensory work; adapted ICT & access technology; flexible use of FF&E
Physical disability PD	Learning and mobility aids, scribe, adapted ICT, communication aids, assistive technology; use of hoists, mobility aids; occupational, physio- & hydrotherapy; personal carers, nurse, medical and/or health care support	Higher accessibility standards; much bulky mobility equipment (independent or assisted use), equipment store, storage bays off corridors; H&S risk assessments: manual handling; shallow pitch stairs, rest places; hygiene & infection control; assisted emergency escape, evacuation lifts & safe refuges; space for carers & equipment storage; place for rest & respite; large equipment storage spaces	Learning & communication aids, adapted ICT, assistive technology; scribe, assistant, carers, occupational therapist; specialist adjustable height FF&E; equipment storage; movement & circulation (some bulky mobility aids)

F